BLACK, NOT DUTCH

"How timely! M. William Howard's Black, Not Dutch offers a fine-grained account of "the challenge of black leadership" in an American Protestant church from the perfect vantage point of an insider. The 1970s were at once so different from the present time, yet so similar in its domestic and international challenges that this book shows how confrontation can produce the much-needed outcome of reconciliation." —*Nell Irvin Painter, Edwards Professor of American History, Emerita, Princeton University*

"The vital phenomenon of black membership in predominantly white denominations continues even in this period of precipitous decline in the membership of mainline Protestant churches. Dr. Howard's narrative of the engagement of black church membership in the RCA from invisibility to prophetic leadership is compelling history with trenchant and sobering gospel truth: There is no reconciliation until we stop lying to one another and can be known for who we really are. Our life together in the body of Christ has profound implications for individual witness, congregational self-reliance, and international struggles for freedom and justice." —*The Reverend Michael Livingston, Interim Senior Minister, The Riverside Church, New York, NY*

"When my 'big brother', Bill Howard, came to work with the Black Council in the RCA in 1972, I was just 14 years old, and today, I am a pastor in this predominantly white denomination. Frequently I ask myself why I keep going, why do I keep serving in this branch of Zion, despite the ongoing struggles that did not end when Dr. Howard went on to become president of New York Theological Seminary. The answer is because I was shaped by the conviction, reflected in Black, Not Dutch, that our faith calls us to authentic reconciliation, and it is a never-ending struggle. (My mentor, Elder Clyde Watts from the Elmendorf Church in East Harlem used to say, "God loves you and so do I.") That is why after all these years I continue to bear witness. And this insightful book, which brings so much of our rich past to light, reminds me of the nobility of our elders and the ground they plowed—just in case I am tempted to forget." —*The Reverend Michael Edwards, Pastor, Dewitt Reformed Church, New York, NY*

"Standing as we are at the threshold of a future with infinite possibilities, Black, Not Dutch is a reminder of the need to step back and take a long, hard look at 'how we got over'. As George Santayana wrote, 'those who cannot remember the past are condemned to repeat it'. Dr. Howard has given a valuable gift to the Reformed Church in America, reminding us of the road we have trod and providing a road map for our moving forward together in a changing world." —*The Reverend Dwayne Jackson, co-pastor with his wife, The Reverend Anna Jackson, Second Reformed Church, Hackensack, NJ*

BLACK, NOT DUTCH

THE REFORMED CHURCH IN AMERICA'S RESPONSE TO THE BLACK MANIFESTO

≠≠≠≠≠≠≠≠≠≠≠≠≠≠≠≠≠≠≠≠≠≠≠≠≠≠≠≠≠≠≠≠≠≠≠≠≠

M. WILLIAM HOWARD, JR.

AFRICA WORLD PRESS
TRENTON | LONDON | CAPE TOWN | NAIROBI | ADDIS ABABA | ASMARA | IBADAN | NEW DELHI

AFRICA WORLD PRESS
541 West Ingham Avenue | Suite B
Trenton, New Jersey 08638

Cover art: Adam Turner Howard
Cover design: Ashraful Haque
Book design: Lemlem Taddese

Cataloging-in-Publication Data may be obtained from the Library of Congress.

ISBNs: 978-1-56902-670-0 (HB)
        978-1-56902-671-7 (PB)

To Nida E. Thomas, who introduced me to the Black Council, and to the Second Generation of Black Council leaders who have caught the vision of the founding elders.

TABLE OF CONTENTS

FOREWORD

This manuscript was completed in 1986. It is meant to capture a time and developments of the period from 1969 to that year, so there has been no effort to contemporize the text to conform with later developments. And if on occasion what is written feels somewhat dated, it may well be, but by intention.

There have been many changes since the original writing: The Black Council became the African American Council, and sometime in the early to mid-2000s, the role of the Council was altered significantly by the denomination. Apartheid ended in South Africa, and the late Reverend James Seawood, a Staten Island pastor formerly on the staff of New Brunswick Seminary, was elected the second African-American president of The General Synod. The Southern Normal School closed, as did a number of other Black boarding schools in the South.

The RCA moved its headquarters from New York City to Grand Rapids, Michigan. Had this happened prior to 1969, it is quite likely that the story told here would never have transpired, because the denomination may not have been confronted by the proponents of the Black Manifesto if its headquarters had not been at the Interchurch Center in New York, where much of the action was focused.

New Brunswick Theological Seminary, whose student body was overwhelmingly white in 1969, has been populated mainly by non-white students for several years, and at this writing is led by an African-American president. This writer left the staff of the Reformed Church in America (RCA) to assume the presidency of New York Theological Seminary in 1992; and Sonia P. Omulepu, the administrative assistant and a key actor in the work of the Black Council, later joined the staff of the World Council of Churches' New York office.

The events recorded in *Black, Not Dutch* occurred in a national environment much different from the one we know now. In 1969, the nation was riding on the waves born of a social movement, clamoring for racial and economic justice, as well as a new American identity. Today, however, the advancements made toward human rights and anti-racism are under attack, with all the assumptions about what America wanted to become being challenged from the highest authorities in the nation.

At the same time, it is noteworthy that the demand for Reparations, signaled in the Black Manifesto, is rising again, this time in the discourse of mainstream politics, and being supported by candidates for public office.

The fact that this is being published now is the result of Sara M. Smith's and Sonia P. Omulepu's belief in its importance for future generations.

PREFACE

The Reformed Church in America (RCA) is the oldest Protestant Church in the United States. It was brought to North America over 350 years ago by Dutch settlers, who had, planted deep in their psyches, the terror and the persecution of the Spanish Inquisition. From that time to this, the church has served as a vehicle of Dutch culture in the "New World." Because of its strong association with the Netherlands in its early days and because of the ethnic character that it has maintained ever since, the "Dutch" Reformed Church, as it was called until 1867, has had limited appeal outside of the Dutch-American community.

It is largely because of this ethnic self-understanding that the RCA, unlike several other predominantly Euro-American churches, did not have substantive contact with Black people. This changed, however, when Black people began moving, in the 1950s, into communities in the older American cities where Reformed Church congregations were located.

Thus, the predominantly Black congregation in the RCA is a phenomenon of the last three decades (1950s–1970s), so the implications of the coming together of these two peoples are yet to be fully examined. In his 1978 book, *Black People and the Reformed Church in America*, Noel L. Erskine began to offer some insight into the vastly different backgrounds from which the Afro-American and the Dutch-American communities emerged. They each have a rich cultural heritage, and religious faith figures prominently in the lives of both. But there is little in their divergent social circumstances to suggest that they would one day worship together in the same denomination. Yet, today, they are. And *Black, Not Dutch* aims to pick up where Erskine left off, by looking more closely at the subsequent decade, a time when the Black Council was coming of age as the collective voice of Black RCA members.

Founded in 1969 as part of the denomination's response to the Black Economic Development Conference's *Black Manifesto*, the Black Council became the first forum in which Black members of the church could clarify the aspirations of the Black community and air them to the larger denomination. For several years prior to the founding of the Black Council, dating back at least to the issuance of the *Credo on Race Relations* in 1957, the RCA sought to speak on the side of justice and equal rights for Black people in society, especially by action of its General Synod. However, there is little evidence that Black people, as RCA members, spoke out on national and international racial justice issues before 1969. To put it succinctly: before 1969, whites spoke on behalf of Black people; after 1969 Blacks spoke for themselves.

This volume will focus primarily on the work of the Black Council. And this will be done by looking at the stance of the denomination regarding the racial climate in the nation before the Black Council was organized; by addressing the question of congregational development in the Black community in the early fifties; and by assessing how the RCA dealt with the question of South Africa and its racist apartheid system before 1969. This approach will help put the Black Council and the issues it has advocated into a more illuminating context.

Above all, though, this will be a story about people, especially Black people, who have seized an opportune moment, produced rather accidentally by a dramatic human confrontation, and turned it into a journey towards faithfulness and towards reconciliation. Most of the leaders of the Black Council are lay people, who never would have thought of themselves as church leaders at the national level. But through prayer, and through a deep faith that their calling is the Lord's work, they have managed not only to persevere but to do so with distinction and with an exciting vision of what the future holds.

This is the labor of so many people and there is no way to give adequate praise to all who deserve it. But a special word must go to Nida Thomas, the person who introduced me to the Black Council in June 1972; to the late B. Moses James; and to David E. Beale, Sara M. Smith, Earle N.S. Hall, and Charles Wagner. The latter four persons have been leaders of the Black Council, and each one brought to the Council what it needed at the time. To the founding elders who took responsibility for calling the first meeting together in the summer of 1969, a special word of commendation is due. In very real terms, it has been their counsel, their patience, and their unrelenting dedication to the work of the organization that has kept me going in difficult times.

I also owe a word of gratitude to Princeton Theological Seminary for generously providing me a place to work in Speer Library and to Sonia P. Omulepu, my assistant for over a decade, who has not only provided technical help for this project, but who, in her own right, believed enough in its urgency to keep encouraging me to do it.

There are no suitable words to express, as fully as I feel, appreciation for my family's understanding and support for this and all the other work I do. Because they too believe in "the mission," the demands are met with ease and grace.

Finally, to the reader I say, it is my singular hope that what has been written on the following pages will play some small part in bridging the tremendous gulf of understanding that exists between two great traditions—one Black, and one Dutch.

INTRODUCTION

Historically, we are an ethnic church. From our forefathers we have inherited Dutch culture and church life. To some degree, we have lost our ethnic character. Yet we still remain an ethnic church. This pattern has produced a high sense of denominational loyalty. Many of our most ethnically integrated churches have exemplified a remarkable sense of fidelity to the enterprises of the Reformed Church in America. These ethnic churches have embodied a solidarity of life and work which have made them distinctive in their communities; for the ethnic church possesses a marked sense of sociological cohesiveness. While contributing to distinctiveness and fostering denominational loyalty, ethnic cohesion can at the same time contribute to an attitude of irresponsibility to the heterogeneous members of the community. Here lies one of the reasons why the ethnic church has found it difficult to adjust to an environment-in-transition. When the ethnic church faces the mounting pressure of an aggressive heterogeneity, it usually becomes more interrelated or moves to a more congenial location.

One of the historical reasons why our church retained its ethnic character was fear; fear of the loss of sociological and ecclesiastical identity in an alien environment. No longer do we need to fear loss of identity, but fear dies hard. We sympathize with the problems involved when an ethnic church experiences the tension between its traditional culture pattern and the compulsion of the compassionate Christ. We commend these churches for their contributions to the life of the denomination, past and present. We now urge them to consider sincerely, the question: Can an ethnically oriented church maintain the luxury of its position under the pressure of modern sociological conditions in the light of the Christian concept of reconciliation?

—*From the 1955 Report of the Committee on Social Welfare to the General Synod of the Reformed Church in America*

Unlike a number of the so-called mainline, predominantly white denominations, the Reformed Church in America did not establish and sustain a persisting relationship with the Black community after the Emancipation Proclamation. This is part of the reason why the church is still, with the encouragement of her Black members, trying to understand how best to take into account the religious heritage and the human aspirations of people of African descent in this largely Dutch-oriented denomination. By saying that the RCA is engaged in this exercise is not to say that she has made any less progress in this regard than her sister churches that are also predominantly white, because virtually all predominantly white denominations have problems responding effectively and consistently to the needs of their Black members, even after having related to them for a century or more.

Most of these denominations, though, have had the benefit of calling upon Black leadership from within their ranks to help them address the race-related problems they faced. This has not been an option for the RCA, since contact between the two peoples was initiated so recently.

One reason why contact between Black folks and the RCA has been so scant and nebulous, according to Erskine, is because the RCA was so beset by internal problems that it did not reach out to Blacks, feeling this would only complicate matters further. Also, there were practically no Black persons in the denomination, hence, no urging for it to become involved in the Black community.[1]

There was one notable exception to this latter obstacle recorded in Erskine's book, and this was the case of Rev. William L. Johnson. Rev. Johnson, according to the records of the General Synod, was a graduate of New Brunswick Theological Seminary and, for several years in the late 1890s, he tried to persuade the Synod to support his work among Black people in Orangeburg, South Carolina and surrounding areas. Rev. Johnson was clearly a determined man, who vigorously sought the affirmation of his work by the RCA. But the RCA was just as determined in rejecting his invitation for it to affiliate itself with his effort.[2] The churches that Johnson founded, after a brief period under the care of the Classis of Philadelphia, were turned over to the old Southern Presbyterian Church.[3]

According to Erskine, prior to Johnson, there is little evidence of contact between the Black community and the Reformed Church in America except through the church's participation in the Slave Trade. In 1855, Samuel B. How presented a paper to the General Synod in defense of slavery. In 1856, John Van Dyke presented a rebuttal of How's position, but after that there is hardly any reference to the plight of Black people in America by the RCA, except for the Reverend Johnson's efforts, until the mid-1950s.[4]

---

1   Noel Leo Erskine, *Black People and the Reformed Church in America* (New York, 1978), p. 45.

2   Ibid., p. 60.

3   The Southern Presbyterian Church became the Presbyterian Church in the United States, based in Atlanta, Georgia, before reuniting in 1983 with the United Presbyterian Church — previously the church's northern wing. The churches divided over the issue of slavery in the 19th century.

4   Erskine, op. cit.

The denomination issued the *Credo on Race Relations* in 1957 (see Appendix 1). This was a time that coincided with two important developments in American society: (1) The Montgomery Bus Boycott and the emerging leadership of Martin Luther King, Jr., and (2) the increasing movement of Black people into formerly all-white residential areas in the North. No doubt, the denomination felt some responsibility to speak out on what was becoming a major social and moral issue for the nation, and the *Credo* could also help clarify for Black persons thinking of joining the RCA, where the church stood, in theory at least, on the matter of racial justice.

BLACK CONGREGATIONS EMERGE

If one of the reasons the RCA did not address the problems of Black people during most of its history was because there was no Black leadership within its ranks pointing the way, then the rise of the predominantly Black congregation was destined to become the beginning of something the denomination had never experienced or fully anticipated. Soon Black members would, if only by their physical presence in churches, become a factor to be considered in the larger RCA agenda.

The origin of the predominantly Black congregation is a direct outgrowth of the "white flight" from major, older American cities to the sprawling suburbs in the 1950s and the growing Black population in the North resulting from the Great Migration from the South. Black people lacked the resources, the contacts, the inclination, and the right color to qualify for the government-guaranteed loans that were needed to buy or build in the cities' outlying areas. So they had to "make do" with moving into those areas that whites were deserting. These "new" areas were often not as run-down as the places Blacks were leaving, so to them this represented progress.

The Black "new arrivals" were often dedicated churchgoers, but they found the commute back to churches in their old neighborhoods too demanding. They therefore explored places to worship nearby where they now lived. What they usually found was a white Protestant church with a declining membership—a membership of whites too poor to move or not yet ready to attach themselves to a church closer to their new homes. Blacks were usually greeted by a relatively friendly white minister in these churches, and this friendly white minister is what Black RCA members of that time remember most about their first encounter with the denomination.

It is no wonder that this would be an outstanding part of their memory of coming to a white-dominated church because, just as it may have been a new experience for the white congregation, it was also a major new venture for the Blacks.

Eleven o'clock on Sunday morning had long been established in North and South alike as "the most segregated hour in America." It took great courage for a Black family to venture out and to attend church at a congregation of an unfamiliar white denomination.

After all, the Black church was the only collectively owned and controlled institution that Black people had built and sustained. It was the birthplace of so many vital enterprises that have benefitted the Black community. It had been the seat of Black-owned publishing companies and insurance firms. It had been and remains the seat of Black political power and the strongest advocate of education within the Black community. So, to even think of severing one's ties with such a heritage even partially was a giant step. And this is what joining a white church means for Black people. Being greeted by people who are overtly friendly helped ease the Black person's entry into this new, "foreign" world. Moreover, this transition was made easier by the Black person's unswerving belief, in spite of centuries of experience to the contrary, that if a church claimed faith in Jesus Christ, it had to make a place in its heart and in its pews for them.

This is a hint of the manner in which many Black people came into contact with the RCA; but Black people have various reasons for joining organizations, and joining the RCA was no exception. Some looked forward enthusiastically to being a part of a new-found church because they wanted to escape the world of the traditional Black church. Some openly said that they were tired of the multiple offerings during the worship service and that they wanted to be kept in church no more than an hour of Sunday morning.

Others were attracted to the community-service programs and ministry to the "total person" that they saw in some congregations. Some wanted to hear sermons preached by "educated" clergy. Their interests varied. Generally speaking, though, there is little indication that Black people, when beginning their association with the RCA, took time to evaluate whether the tradition they were bringing with them contrasted with the tradition they were encountering. Some individuals may have taken stock of this privately, but there was no apparent in-depth effort by Black people as a group to understand this. This may be because Blacks joined the church as individuals and questions of group identity had not yet been raised.

Because of their fundamentally different views of God, because of the function of religion in the lives of both groups, and because of the distinct ecclesiastical polity to which each group had been accustomed, the examination of variances in these traditions remains part of the unfinished business of the denomination. There is also no indication, as we shall see later, that Blacks analyzed for themselves the nature of race relations in the church in this early period. It seemed not to occur to the Black RCA members who entered the church in the fifties that the same white members who were so warm and friendly in church were also rapidly moving away from their now racially mixed neighborhoods.

A Black elder in a New York City church recalls reading the

minutes of his church's consistory, dated 1950, when the church was facing racial transition in the neighborhood where it was located. The question of whether the church would make an intentional effort to reach out to the newly arrived Blacks was put to a vote. The consistory voted Yes, although by a small margin. Nonetheless, this white consistory had the foresight to act upon a fact of life that was already upon them. A result of this decision was the employment of a Black student to assist the white pastor in outreach work. This Black student was Wilbur Washington from New Brunswick Theological Seminary. Years later, Dr. Washington would serve as the first full-time Black member of the seminary faculty and as the first Black president of the RCA's General Synod. Four years after Washington's student days, The Rev. James Thomas was installed as the first Black pastor of New York's Mott Haven Reformed Church, at a time when the church's membership was still predominantly white.[5]

The racial transition that was so evident in the Mott Haven section of the Bronx was also happening in other places where the RCA had a long-standing presence, but it was not until the late fifties that concern about how the church might best deal with this transition began to surface on the national level. By that time there were at least 16 RCA churches known to be experiencing racial transition.[6] The transition in most places, however, was not dealt with in as forthright a manner as it had been at Mott Haven. Rather, change in the racial composition of churches simply drifted, with no plan of action that took the churches' changing demographics into account.

At the very time that white flight from the inner cities was

5   Ibid.
6   From July 8, 1983, interviews with the Black Council's founding elders: Clyde Watts, John Ashley, and Edgar Dillard.

8

at its peak, the denomination was issuing public statements in favor of open housing and racially integrated communities. There was no lack of insight into the problem, just a lack of will, as the following excerpt from the minutes of the 1960 General Synod will show:

> ...discrimination in housing has limited our enjoyment of stable interracial Christian fellowship and has in fact limited us to being or becoming segregated churches. The pattern has been that once vested real estate and money interests have opened a community to non-white occupancy, the panic of the whites and the tremendous housing needs of the non-whites have been the occasion by which a parish area just became negro and thereby the church segregated.[7]

Perspectives like these were persistently kept before the denomination, year after year during this period, by both the Christian Action Commission and the by that time defunct Board of Domestic Missions. They were apparently inspired in their views by Christian conviction.[8] But at the same time that their dogged determination did not allow them to accept the principles of racially segregated churches, these denominational bodies also failed to help the RCA come to grips with the fact that segregation was a *fait accompli* as Blacks moved in.

This segregation was due to the flight of white RCA members. The existence of segregation on the one hand, and the reluctance to accept the fact of segregated churches by some on the other, helped to paralyze the RCA and to thwart what motivation it may have had to deal with the transition situation it faced. It is in this state of immobilization and classic

---

7   *Minutes of the General Synod,* 1959 (New York), p. 208.

8   Ibid., 1969, p. 179.

ambivalence that we can see why more was not done to encourage the development of Black ordained leadership in the denomination. To openly promote the development of Black clergy was to concede that race was a factor to be considered in church leadership.

A good deal of the energy of advocates of fair treatment for Blacks was spent in promoting the idea that race should not be a factor in church affairs. They argued forcefully, moreover, that, in the Christian community, race should not be a factor in human relations *per se*. To challenge this argument, particularly if you were Black, was to risk being regarded as a troublemaker with Black nationalist (and therefore un-Christian) tendencies.

Even Black church members looked upon such Black persons as stirring up trouble; the latter group preferred to downplay the plight of the larger Black community, hoping they had found a place of refuge from constantly encountering the race issue. This delusion was made more plausible by the fact that Blacks, normally expecting cool-to-hostile treatment from whites, met whites in the RCA who were outwardly friendly toward them.

Another dimension of this problem was the paternalism and dependence that often characterized the church's ministry. The fleeing white members had had an ethnic identification with the church most of their lives. This was also the basis of their financial commitment to the church, so their leaving often resulted in a financial dependence by the church on regional RCA judicatories, and on "friends" across judicatory lines.

In order to keep the doors of these transitional churches open, it was not unusual for their white ministers to seek help for their ministries in the same way that "faith missionaries" to foreign countries sought help in underwriting their work.

At the time, this probably seemed like the most effective and prudent thing to do. But, in hindsight, one wonders whether, in order to make the work attractive to potential (white) supporters, it had to be promoted in a way that was non-threatening to whites and often demeaning to Blacks. Keep in mind that most white donors were likely to have had no experience in relating to Black people as peers, and they probably had little or no direct knowledge of Black religious heritage.

Black RCA members at the time appeared ignorant of or at least aloof from much of what was going on in the streets, so they served as an antidote for anxious white RCA members who were witnessing the rising tide of Black protest every night on the "six o'clock news." If the white minister, and a select few from his Black congregation, took the case for financial support to their potential donors, the non-threatening nature of the encounter could be assured.

While this arrangement may have worked well in the early days of the Black RCA congregation, it has proven detrimental in the long run. This is true because what may have been a stopgap measure for survival then has turned out to be an entrenched pattern of dependence today. This pattern is still having its harmful effects on Black RCA members. It has left them, until recently, without a strong drive for Black lay and clerical leadership and it has left most of the churches they attend dependent on judicatories and "friendly churches" for their very survival. None seem to have questioned this way of supporting churches in increasingly all Black communities before the RCA was confronted with the *Black Manifesto* in 1969.

When the Black Caucus (the "general assembly" of Black RCA members) met that year to organize the first Black Council, the bitterness and frustration shown by some in attendance was a by-product of the many unanswered questions that had been left to fester to the point of exploding over the years. Prior to this, there is no record of concern for

11

racial justice being expressed at the denominational level by Black RCA members. These concerns had been aired entirely by white-led committees, with little or no involvement by the Black members. Black people had been silent too long. They were overdue to speak out from their own direct experience of racial oppression.

They had no denominational identity, and they had very little knowledge and experience of how things worked in the church. After almost twenty years, there was still little understanding of the church's ecclesiastical roots and its theological tradition. Leading Black members of consistories had never even read the basic text of church government, *The Book of Church Order.*

Most of them had had life-long church affiliations, but they seemed willing to abandon all they had brought with them into the RCA in order to fit into their new-found church. This is not to say they made a conscious decision to do this, but they went along with things willy-nilly, accepting as inevitable the fact that their heritage would not be nurtured by the white pastor.

This state of affairs existed because there was no open, honest discussion about the implications of the RCA's contact with this group of people from such a different religious tradition. In the mid-1960s, Blacks began to have doubts about the efficacy of racial integration as a means of obtaining justice for Black people, especially when they understood that white advocates of integration expected Blacks to adopt a white cultural orientation and generally to strive for acceptance on white terms. This model of integration was at work in the RCA. "The Changing City Challenges the Church," a theme that was to be celebrated on November 1, 1963, in observance of North American Missions Sunday, [9] would have been a good forum

---

9   Elders' interviews.

in which to analyze these and other issues, but apparently the chance was missed.

If it can be said that the whites who had their own vision of Black involvement in the RCA actually obstructed Black leadership development and prolonged the dependence of Black congregations on white benefactors, then the first wave of Black members coming into these churches were collaborators in this ill-fated enterprise. Blacks and whites both lacked the foresight to understand that a survival plan, adopted in the beginning stages of transition, could not become a permanent *modus operandi*. Perhaps the challenge to Black congregants of ending dependence upon willing and able supporters was too great, and the challenge to white churchgoers of expecting more from the financially less able group was too risky.

Black people also seemed willing to carry the burden of racial segregation, even though segregated neighborhoods and churches were the result of white flight. One gets this impression because Blacks seemed not to object to being pawns for whites in order to make a point with their RCA counterparts. One group of whites wanted to show to the other that Blacks and whites could live and work together. And they were determined to prove this without regard for the Black community's right and power to choose options that whites did not dictate or approve.

Their (collective) opposite number was those whites who felt the RCA should not remain in the changing communities but should follow its traditional constituency to the suburbs.[10] Given the position of this latter group, Black members wound up supporting those who advocated remaining, lest they appear to endorse the views of those who might be rejecting Black people for racist reasons. Because of the pathology

---

10 *Minutes of the General Synod,* 1963, p. 91.

induced by racism, Black people are sometimes ready to embrace whites who show any sign of friendliness, without much analysis. In the RCA today, there are Black persons who still feel beholden to whites for this reason.

BEFORE THE BLACK COUNCIL

When the *Credo on Race Relations* was issued in 1957, it marked the RCA's official entry into the world of race relations. While there had been several reports issued on the growing number of interracial congregations, the impetus for the *Credo* seemed as much related to events outside the church as to the growth of the church's Black membership. The *Credo* could not expect to have much impact on the movement for racial justice in society, but, in practical terms, it also had no dramatic impact on the status or participation of Black members in the affairs of the church.

The Montgomery Bus Boycott began in 1955, when Ms. Rosa Parks refused to give up her seat on a city bus. Then, Martin Luther King, Jr. became leader of the Montgomery Improvement Association. By 1956, because the situation in Montgomery had become so visible to the nation, the RCA felt a need to react, not only to Montgomery, but to the situation in South Africa.[11] South Africa's apartheid system of severe racial separation had been a source of embarrassment and anxiety for the RCA, since apartheid had been implemented in South Africa in 1948. This was due to the common, historical roots that the RCA shared with South Africa's Dutch Reformed churches. Moreover, it had been the Dutch Reformed Church that had provided the spiritual undergirding and the theological *apologia*

---

11   Ibid., 1959, pp. 105-106.

for apartheid. These factors created the broader climate that shaped the *Credo*, but it would be wrong to say that the growing number of Black people in local RCA congregations had no influence on these developments.

The church's public statements on racial justice kept pace with the times throughout the late fifties and the early sixties. The denomination was led in this by the Board of Domestic Mission; by its successor, the Board of North American Missions; and by the Christian Action Commission. Nineteen sixty-two was the first year after the *Credo* was adopted that the topic of the Civil Rights Movement, or race relations in the United States, did not appear in the Christian Action Commission's report to the General Synod. Each time the synod spoke, its message could be linked to some new chapter in the unfolding social crusade that was going on. In 1963, the Christian Action Commission (CAC) called on the RCA to endorse the general direction of the Civil Rights Movement, giving special mention to the Southern Christian Leadership Conference (SCLC). At that Synod, an offering of $696.05 was raised to support SCLC's work. The CAC also urged support for the 1964 Civil Rights Act.

Moreover, it was in 1964 that the Board of North American Missions, no doubt believing that the movement for racial justice was sufficiently urgent on the nation's agenda, called upon the General Synod to establish a Commission on Race that would have the following functions:

1. The preparation and distribution of information and educational materials;
2. The encouraging of each congregation in the RCA to become in fact a living exposition of the affirmations contained in the *Credo on Race Relations*;
3. The giving of aid, encouragement, counsel, and assistance to individual members and churches as they may seek to

witness in difficult situations in the area of Race Relations;
(and)
4. Assisting Particular Synods and/or Classes to establish local
    commissions on Race.[12]

An annual budget of $8,500 was allocated for the
Commission's work, and Howard C. Schade, an executive
secretary for the Board of North American Missions, was
assigned to staff the Commission. Its reports were sent as part
of the Board of North American Missions report to the General
Synod. The CAC served as an advisory body to the
Commission.

The RCA was in a new ball game. It had virtually no direct
experience with the complex questions of Black-white relations.
This became evident later as the Commission was unable to
find any real focus or to provide leadership on the race
question. While it helped to support some positive events and
projects, the Commission was never able to get a substantive
program off the ground. Nevertheless, when it spoke, it spoke
in a supportive voice for the work that was going on in places
like Selma, Alabama, and throughout Mississippi, against legal
segregation.

The first mandate for the Commission lasted two years,
following which it was to make recommendations for action to
the Synod. The work of the Commission was aimed at helping
white RCA members understand and adapt to the changes that
were taking place, not at mobilizing the Black and white
members of the church to actively oppose racism. Even when
action was proposed, the target audience seemed white. An
illustration of this is the first report of the Commission on Race
in 1965, from which the following excerpt is taken:

---

12 Ibid., 1956, p. 166.

...that the General Synod affirm its agreement with the action taken in January 1961, by the North American Area Council of the Alliance of Reformed Churches: There may come a time in spite of efforts to correct, when a law prevails that keeps people from receiving justice and thus conflicts with the purposes of God as they are revealed in the Gospel. At such time, it is our opinion that a Christian, after serious and careful consideration, and after sharing his concerns with other members of the household of faith may engage alone or with others in an act of civil disobedience (if)...his actions are taken first in the spirit of a faithful servant of his faithful Lord, and in sight and knowledge of authorities, and with a full willingness to accept the consequences imposed upon him by the society under existing law.[13]

The same report urges support for those who might encounter difficulties in adhering to the *Credo on Race Relations*. The concern expressed here was for whites who were being criticized because of the controversial positions of equal-rights advocacy they had taken. For the first two years of the Commission's life, there were no Black members. Two Black men, Chester Gray and the Reverend Samuel Williams, served on the Commission after the 1966 General Synod meeting, when the commission was allowed to expand its membership to include two at-large seats.

Today, in hindsight, of course, it is somewhat easier to critique this commission for its shortcomings; but in those days, before public awareness of paternalism and institutionalized racism was as finely tuned as it sometimes is today, perhaps the Commission members were doing the best they could under the circumstances. Nevertheless, the RCA had a choice to speak or not to speak on the questions of racial justice, given how timid and silent its own Black members were about the role the

---

13   Ibid., 1964, p. 96.

church should play in combatting racism. And it did choose to speak.

One wonders what a difference concerted Black involvement in the denomination's deliberations might have had on her actions. Some indications of this came when the Black Council was founded years later. The Council was founded at the end of the Civil Rights era, however, when Richard Nixon's philosophy of "benign neglect" (adopted from Daniel Patrick Moynihan) was beginning to gain currency and the ascendancy of the political right wing was looming on the horizon. From that point on, the Council was operating in a considerably more hostile social and political climate than that which existed just prior to 1968.

The Commission on Race was given a mandate in 1966 to continue for two more years and in 1968, when its continuation was up for discussion again, the General Program Council (GPC) was being created. It was decided that the work of the Commission would become a part of the GPC, but it would continue for a time as a consultant to the new body. As an indication of the Commission's growth in understanding the problems that America faced with racism, note this excerpt from its final report to the General Synod, signed by its chairperson, Professor John W. Beardsley, III:

> It is becoming evident that a basic problem in our country is that of "institutional racism"—the tendency of institutions to support an existing pattern of life whether or not people consciously seek that goal. In the present case our institutions have accommodated themselves to a society that operates to the advantage of the whites and the disadvantage of the blacks in spite of the fact that most people are men and women of good will. To counteract this institutional racism requires changes in the structure of the community, and, as all the informed studies of our cities point out, visible changes

apparent to the victims of discrimination must come quickly if relative peace is to be preserved and harmonious cooperation between Black and white is to be the path by which we work. There have been too few of these changes, and the restlessness that is evident in our cities is part of the result. The church has not, on the whole, shown leadership in this matter. It is of pressing concern that Christians join others in the various community efforts that really make for change through public and private agencies concerned with such matters as fair and decent housing, fair employment, quality education for all and equitable police practice and law enforcement.

The report goes on to say:

One matter of pressing concern is the need to increase the participation of Black people in the life and leadership of the denomination and to be sure that our Black members, like the rest of the community, enjoy the opportunity of identity and growth toward which the old Civil Rights Movement pointed them—an opportunity for identity and growth that motivates such existing movements as that for black power, and that underlies many of the educational changes now going on in our schools and universities.[14]

Clearly, this report by the Commission on Race was meant to promote understanding of Black people's aspirations among white people. This served a constructive purpose, because it was being done in the overwhelmingly white Reformed Church in America. This was the clearest statement of Black aspirations to appear on record in the RCA up to that time. In fact, its characterization of racism and the challenges it presents to the church are still very current. It is unfortunate that this report was not given an official status and promoted in the

---

14   Ibid., 1965, p. 84.

same way as the *Credo on Race Relations*, because it is an excellent updating of the journey that was precipitated in the RCA by the *Credo*. However, the report of this Commission, as it turned out, was overshadowed by another event at the General Synod dealing with the same subject—the *Black Manifesto* (see Appendix 2).

Some of the same principles mentioned in the Beardslee report were reflected in the RCA's response to the *Manifesto*. One reason for this may be that three prominent members of the Commission on Race were also members of the Ad Hoc Committee chosen to draft the response.

THE *BLACK MANIFESTO*: CATALYST FOR A NEW ERA

It can be said that the Reformed Church in America had been relatively aloof from many of the struggles against white racism in America, but 1969 represented a profound break with that past. When the Black Economic Development Conference (BEDC) representatives took over the offices of the RCA at 475 Riverside Drive in New York, neither Black nor white church members could have anticipated what this would mean for the future.

Before addressing the particular experience of the Reformed Church in America, let us focus on the context into which this *Black Manifesto* was presented. The church's actions fit into a broader picture.

In writing about James Forman's interruption of church services at New York's Riverside Church to present the *Black Manifesto* on May 4th of that year, Gayraud S. Wilmore says:

> ...confrontation did not so much precipitate a crisis among the nation's churches and synagogues, as it revealed a crisis which had already existed in those major denominations for at least three years prior to Forman's return from SNCC obscurity. This crisis was about the depth and seriousness of the Black revolution in America. Second, it stems from an enervating battle fatigue among the liberal churches that had fought for civil rights. And third, that crisis comes from the

fact that these churches, since 1966, had shown little enthusiasm for or commitment to the goals of the Black power movement.[15]

The Black Power Movement was the outgrowth of at least a decade of intense confrontation with racism, in its legal and extra-legal manifestations, by a relatively small group of committed individuals known as the Student Non-Violent Coordinating Committee (SNCC). "SNICK," as it became widely known, functioned as an interracial body in some of the most dangerous places in the South. Its members lived among the victims of racism and poverty and they reflected their needs and aspirations. Sometimes the needs of the poor and the marginalized with whom SNCC members worked did not square with what the Establishment wanted or expected, so SNCC members were constantly at the center of controversy, and their lives were often in danger. Stokely Carmichael, the person widely credited with popularizing the concept of "Black Power," was a leader of SNCC. A number of those listed as members of the BEDC were former SNCC activists.

The call for Black Power offended many whites (and Blacks too) because it identified empowerment of the Black community as a key to Black liberation in America. Black empowerment, while it did not exclude whites in quite the way its antagonists claimed, would depend largely on the efforts of Black people, working for themselves and cooperating with one another. This goal was compatible with the reality of the Black condition in America and it accepted an understanding of Black people's predicament much as Black nationalists had defined it. Black Power advocates called upon Black people to reject integration with whites, as a primary strategy of the movement for justice. Rejecting integration, however, meant excluding the

---

15 Ibid., 1969, pp. 84-85.

views and the contributions of whites and Blacks who were prominent in the Civil Rights Movement.

No attempt will be made here to analyze the faults of the "integrationist era," but suffice it to say, its fundamental flaws were becoming more and more evident as the end of the decade of the 1960s approached.

The limits of white leadership over Blacks in the struggle also became more evident. This state of affairs provoked the question, "What is the white person's role in the anti-racism struggle?" Few bother to recall that, when Carmichael and his associates challenged the Black community to focus their energies on the attainment of Black power, they also appealed to whites who were committed to combatting racism to return to their own communities and help to fight racism there.

Some whites took up this challenge, but others were alienated from the movement because they could not adapt to the leading Black personalities. Some conceded that they had little chance of changing the hearts and the conduct of their relatives and friends.

The Black Power Movement was an important chapter in a long movement for Black liberation. This movement began in 1619, when the first ships carrying African slaves arrived in North America. The demand for Black power grew out of the experience of people struggling together. It was not a frivolous development, but one which came after much pain and intense human interaction. It also was not the only new dimension to be added to the old Civil Rights agenda.

Towards the end of his life, Dr. King himself began openly to express doubts about certain of the Civil Rights Movement's previous assumptions. He questioned particularly whether freedom for Black people could be achieved simply by moving a few chairs around the deck of a sinking ship. In an April 4, 1967 sermon at New York's Riverside Church, he said that materialism, racism, and militarism were so deeply ingrained in America that it would take a "Revolution of Values" to create the change that was needed.

In the Riverside Church sermon, Dr. King also made his most well-publicized pronouncement against the Vietnam War. In that address, he drew a clear connection between the plight of Black people in the USA and that of people of color in other parts of the world. In addition to his concern about Vietnam, he expressed specific concern about events in Central America and South Africa.

Even before Dr. King began to speak out consistently on international issues, SNCC had become conscious of the global dimension of the struggle for freedom. The international issue that is thought to have caused the most trouble for SNCC was its identification with the cause of the Palestinians in the Middle East. American supporters of Israel began to withdraw their support for Civil Rights activists. Pressures were brought to bear upon other Civil Rights organizations to isolate SNCC and to counter SNCC's position on the Palestinian issue and other "radical" topics. This marked the beginning of the much-talked-about political tension between Blacks and Jews that is still evident today.

This background lends support to the fact that what was originally seen as a domestic movement for the fair treatment of Blacks was unfolding into a much more complicated, protracted movement that threatened to shake the foundations of the nation. Those who had a limited view of this movement were growing weary and confused. Erstwhile white liberals were becoming increasingly conservative. Some won elective office or otherwise advanced their careers by capitalizing on their "change of heart" regarding the anti-racism struggle. Still others simply shaved, took a bath and eased back into the Establishment from which they had come. Things were getting more entangled. Too much seemed to be at stake. Instead of dealing with a proverbial wart, they were dealing with a case of terminal cancer.

By 1969, the anger of the urban ghetto (especially in the North) that erupted after the assassination of Dr. King revealed just how deep-seated the bitterness caused by deferred dreams really was. White church groups that had worked closely with Civil Rights leaders began to rethink their involvement. The implications of radical change in America, of the kind which many agreed was needed, might cost too much.

This is the climate that Gayraud Wilmore was writing about. It was a climate that grew out of the tried and tested remedies of a turbulent time and the experience of excluded and bruised peoples who were not yet satisfied.

The efforts and the intentions of the Christian churches were not only being called into question; they were being identified as part of the problem. Instead of being praised for their past actions and statements, they were being criticized for half-heartedness—for being long on words and pledges and short on concrete action. The *Black Manifesto* focused upon the wealth that had been accumulated within a system that profited from the exploitation of Black labor. Hence the *Manifesto*'s demands for reparations.

The *Black Manifesto* was aimed at churches and synagogues, and it was meant as a moral challenge. Its proponents knew that reparations for past injustices had a strong basis in history (the early advocates of Affirmative Action justified their position as being a step towards reparations). The demand was that religious institutions pay reparations to Black people for their two centuries under forced slavery *and* for an additional hundred years of servitude to racist institutions.

After the *Manifesto* was made public, religious leaders found it difficult to remain neutral on the issue. A stream of endorsements and denunciations came from Blacks and whites. Most were predictable. A few institutions responded by actually sending money to the BEDC. Most merely expressed thanksgiving to God for the challenge that the *Black Manifesto* presented.[16] The Reformed Church in America was among the latter group.

The national offices of the Reformed Church were "liberated" by James Forman and his associates on June 5, 1969, and thus became the first of several to be occupied at the Interchurch Center in New York in the campaign for reparations. On June 6, 1969, Mr. Forman was invited to address the RCA's General Synod, then in session at New Brunswick, New Jersey. It was his address to the General Synod and the Synod's response that resulted in the founding of the Black Council.

Several crucial matters were addressed at that meeting having to do with the future mission of the RCA, but none competed for drama with the appearance of James Forman. Some delegates seemed prepared for Forman's visit. Some Black and white persons, understanding that Mr. Forman's appearance at that meeting would have a significant impact on race relations in the denomination, attempted to position themselves (in the words of one person directly involved in this historic development) to "pull Mr. Forman's chestnut out of the fire." There were no identifiable Black voices in the RCA calling for a favorable response to the *Black Manifesto*, but some had ideas about how Forman's intervention could be exploited.

In its report to the Synod, the "Ad Hoc Committee to Respond to the Black Manifesto" recommended that a Black

---

16 Gayraud S. Wilmore, "The Church's Response to the *Black Manifesto*" (A mimeographed paper circulated by the UPUSA, 1969).

Council be established and that it be given $100,000 to spend in any way it saw fit.

This recommendation and several others were adopted by the Synod. However, at no time did the newly established Black Council show an interest in passing this grant on to the BEDC. Instead, as persons present at the organizing meeting of the Council recall, several proposals were offered, suggesting how the $100,000 could be used in Black communities. Subsequently, the Council voted not to accept money from the RCA for independent grant-making and this decision was pivotal in determining the nature of the Black Council's role and mission in the church.

From the outset, the Black elders who were delegates to the 1969 General Synod felt that the Synod's primary motivation for establishing the Black Council was to create a "buffer" between itself and the BEDC. The elders believed that by calling a Black Council into being, the General Synod was putting Black RCA members in a position of having to deal directly with Mr. Forman, thus relieving the church at large of that responsibility. One of these elders recalled that the first person to speak following the adoption of the Response to the *Black Manifesto* was a white man who asked the Black General Synod delegates "what _they_ were going to do" to get Mr. Forman out of the RCA headquarters.

This disposition confirmed the elder's feeling that the church was not as concerned about the issues raised by the *Manifesto* as it was about Forman's vacating the church headquarters.

Second-guessing the motivations of those who voted to adopt the "Response to the Black Manifesto" in 1969 is risky business. Perhaps many voted out of a genuine commitment to justice. But the level of confidence was sufficiently low among the three founding elders of the Council to make them question

29

the church's motives.

The need for a buffer is still the presumed motive for establishing the Black Council and it informs the Black Council's self-understanding to this day. Many Blacks have yet fully to believe that the RCA regards the Council as much more than a buffer, whose value to the denomination rises and falls according to the tide of public concern about racism in society.

Whether accurate or not, this self-understanding did not deter the Council from seizing the opportunity precipitated by this "accident of history" to galvanize Black people in the denomination and to convert this disruption of business-as-usual in the church into an authentic expression of faithfulness to the Gospel of Jesus Christ. Out of the shock and confusion of its early days, the Black Council was able to establish sound goals and priorities based upon the needs of Black RCA members.

The 1969 Black Caucus elected the first Black Council. It was convened that August by John A. Ashley, Edgar Dillard, and Clyde Watts, three of the four Black elders present at that year's synod. The fourth elder, Willard Moore, did not attend the August meeting, even though he apparently agreed with the notion of creating the Council. According to Elder Ashley, who remained in touch with Mr. Moore, Moore considered it inappropriate to attend the organizing meeting, since he did not enjoy the support of his otherwise all-white congregation. It has been reported that his resignation from the church a short time afterwards may have been precipitated by his church's failure to support the founding of the Black Council.[17]

Elder Clyde Watts presided over the first Black Caucus meeting, and for the first time in RCA's history, Black RCA

---

17   Robert S. Lecky and H. Elliott Wright, *Black Manifesto: Religion, Racism and Reparations*, p. 17.

members had embarked on a journey to establish their identity in the "oldest Protestant church in America."

What Watts remembers most about this meeting was the anger displayed by Black people from different parts of the church. Whites present at the meeting were seeing for the first time, he believed, the depth of feeling that Black people harbored.

They also witnessed their confusion. The name, "*Black*" Council, for example, was opposed by some. That this name prevailed as the name of the new Council was no easy achievement. Some held out for the "Christian" Council; some the "Minority" Council. Anything but the "*Black*" Council. This illustrated how Black people have been taught, by various means over several centuries, to be reluctant to affirm themselves.

Prayer was the mainstay of the Council's formation, and the founding elders credit prayer with leading the Council towards some of its most important initial decisions. Perhaps the most crucial decision was its acceptance of B. Moses James's recommendation that it not accept a grant-making role. The Caucus was not to be a vehicle for "absolving the guilt of white RCA members" for their complicity in creating, maintaining, and benefitting from a racist society. The $100,000 that the General Synod voted to grant the new organization could hardly make a dent in the tremendous needs that existed in the Black community.

Refusing to be a distributor of "conscience" money on behalf of the RCA and insisting on Black people's full participation in the decision-making process at every level of the denomination, the Black Council gave notice that it would focus on substance.

The Council did not hire an executive for its first three years, even though funds were available almost immediately for this purpose. The members wanted to be sure they knew where they wanted to go and what kind of executive staff person could help them get there.

The Central purpose of the Council is stated in the preamble of its constitution: "To become peers with all other members of the Reformed Church in America." The Council's goals have been set with this purpose in mind. This purpose would appear to be acceptable to all, but not all RCA members have found it easy to embrace.

There was little fanfare in the first meetings of the newly elected Council. The participants were not particularly conscious of the historic significance of their work. Much of the work consisted of mundane chores and frustration. It was their task to find out, for the first time, where Black people worshipped throughout the denomination and to find out what were their concerns. They also had the responsibility of being sure that these concerns and needs were presented to the church for action as needed. This was done completely by volunteers. After almost two decades of dedicated and unrelenting work, the early Council members can now begin to see the long-term value of their endeavors.

The Council knew that its executive staff person would have to be fully accountable to the organization. Because, in order to be true to the Council's purpose of helping Blacks become peers, the executive staff person would have to do some things that would not always be popular or well-understood in the wider denomination. From the beginning, the Council was concerned that Blacks be represented on policy bodies. It wanted to enhance leadership capacity among the clergy and the laity. In order to implement these two major thrusts, long-term work would be required and long-established patterns of behavior would have to be changed. This would prove difficult and controversial at times. Additional priorities have been added to the Black Council's agenda as time has passed but participating in shaping policy and facilitating leadership development remain top priorities of the organization to this day.

HOW THE BLACK COUNCIL DEFINE ITSELF

When the Black Council expressed its determination to assist Blacks in becoming peers in the RCA, this decision was based upon certain assumptions. One is firmly rooted in the Christian Gospel: Reconciliation is central to realizing Christian community. The Council keeps before it the indispensability of reconciliation and what Martin Luther King, Jr. called "the Beloved Community." The Council sees itself as an agent of this Beloved Community.

This will surprise those who have viewed the Council as promoting "racism-in-reverse." When Black RCA members began to meet among themselves to determine how they would tackle the problems they faced, they were labeled "separatist" by some Council critics. The era of respect for the right of self-determination had not yet reached maturity.

In time, it became ever so clear that Black people could not be partners, participating fully and responsibly in the church, if they did not "have their own act together." So the Council's apparent separation, denying whites access to its meetings, gave the more direct victims of racial oppression a chance to contemplate what they must do to respond.

Black people who insisted that the *Black* Caucus *be* Black were very experienced in interracial dialogue. They had background knowledge of how some whites, because of their own racist conditioning, felt a need to be leaders even when Blacks were in the majority. They also knew how defensive some whites became in situations where white racism came under attack. The Council felt it was more important to give Black people a chance to plan their own strategies, even if it meant they would appear anti-white. Those who were critical of this policy chose to ignore the Black Council members and their supporters and to work in interracial situations in most other areas of church life.

Prior to 1969, matters of particular concern to Black people had been addressed in the RCA by whites, for the most part. After two decades of growing involvement in RCA congregations, the Black congregant remained virtually isolated from the mainstream of the RCA. In the Council's view, if this were to change, the church at large would have to encounter the Black member, not as an object of mission, but as a contributing, self-respecting peer. Paternalism was not yet dead, but it was mortally wounded.

While the money was not accepted, the fact that the church had offered $100,000 no doubt helped the early members of the Council take their duties more seriously. The Council was forced to look inward at the problems it faced in the RCA for the first time. Most Black congregations were dependent on support from elsewhere. Black preachers were extremely scarce. There were no seminarians.

Their seriousness was reflected in the role, relationship, and accountability that they chose for the Council's executive director. This staff person would be accountable solely to the Black Council, and his/her basic assignment would be to carry out the decisions of the Council. The new organization sensed what would be required of its director, just as it understood the difficulty of achieving peer relationship for Blacks in the RCA. This relationship of accountability has come under attack by some elements of the denomination ever since the time it was adopted.

In 1969 and 1979, overtures to the General Synod regarding the relationship of "minority council" staff to the denomination (or lack thereof) were construed as attempts to challenge the accountability relationship between the Black Council and its executive director. Controversy over this accountability relationship is what precipitated the creation of the Joint Committee on Relationships and Responsibilities of Minority Councils and Denominational Policy Bodies in 1976.

The Joint Committee produced the first affirmative statement on the value of and the theological basis for councils of racially oppressed groups in the denomination. It also produced the first blueprint for how the decision of 1969 to involve Black people in the denomination's decision-making process would be implemented. The name initially proposed for this Committee was something like the "Committee on Accountability of Minority Councils to Denominational Policy Bodies." However, because of the sensitivity of then General Secretary Marion E. DeVelder, who wanted to be sure that this committee did not appear punitive in its intent, the name was changed. It was his desire to achieve a deeper understanding and a better working relationship among the groups involved and he knew that this could best be done if the General Synod did not appear to be trying to whip the racial minority groups into line.

This conclusion of the Joint Committee represented a new, progressive stride for the RCA in the development of race relations. It is also a tribute to the openness to one another's insights and perspectives shown by members of this committee.

As important as they are, concerns about executive accountability and who could attend Black Council meetings were really just housekeeping matters. Issues like leadership development, Black Christian Education, and the self-reliance of local churches soon became central to the Council's life. These needs emerged in the early discussions, speeches, and writings of Council leaders.

The Council had been understood mostly in political terms. Representing only about one percent of the RCA's membership, though, Black people could hardly hope to have conventional political clout, acting alone. That is why the Council has seen itself as a moral and ethical challenge to the church. This moral and ethical challenge was accepted in 1969 when the church responded to the *Black Manifesto,* and it was accepted again in 1974 when the General Synod reaffirmed its commitment to the *Response to the Black Manifesto.*

The Black Council's existence may not be an expression of the ideal Christian community. It may be true when people say that "racial subgroups" do not represent the best expression of the Christian church. However, the Black Council, the American Indian Council, the Hispanic Council, and the Pacific Asian Council are but reminders that white racism has invaded the church. And since these groups have not been the propagators of white racism, but rather victims of it, the RCA should not deny them the means of defending themselves and of developing their potential.

The RCA committed itself to the existence of Councils and this commitment should be sustained as long as a *de facto* "White Council" exists. The White Council, in this case, is that informal and formal network of white persons who, because of their natural association with one another, are able to shape the outcome of important church policy without people of color having had even the slightest impact. The basis of the Black Council is not exclusively negative, though. There are many positive features.

It is hard to imagine how the relationship of Black people to the RCA, prior to 1969, could have led to "normal" relations between the two "peoples." There is little likelihood that Blacks and whites could have engaged together in true Christian discipleship without building a different relationship. However inadvertently, they had been lying to each other. They were not allowing each other to know their true selves. This may not have been intentional, but the conflicts that actually divide Black people from white people in the larger society were not allowed to come to the surface in the church, where they could have been openly addressed, if not resolved.

The Black Council should be celebrated for its contribution to the different relationship that has developed in the denomination among her Black and white members during the seventies and eighties.

The Black congregation gradually became a sister congregation to all other RCA congregations. The Black member developed a sense of belonging and access to the denomination never before enjoyed. There is also a growing sense of freedom among Black people to affirm the religious heritage that they brought to the RCA. In speaking at the second B. Moses James lecture at Western Seminary in 1976 about the need to reclaim that heritage, Gayraud S. Wilmore said:

> I don't mean to suggest that we forgot we were Black. This is almost impossible to do, no matter how much money or education we may have. I mean that we have learned to suppress blackness as an expressive form of spirituality. We found ourselves operating church like a business or a neighborhood club, rather than enjoying church as an extension of the Black family and a community of friendship and intimacy. We told ourselves that we really didn't need the long prayers and gospel songs, the loud preaching, the emotional congregational responses, the evangelistic revivals, the three or four offerings, the every-time-you-turn-around

money raising events, the all-day-in-church Sundays, the hard-to-get-along-with, autocratic, preacher domination. And perhaps we didn't need all that and should not want it for ourselves or for our children. But that improvised, tangled web of traditional Black church life somehow catches and holds the spirit that made it possible for Black people to feel that they were somebody, to have an identity of their own and to survive the onslaught of poverty, racism and oppression from day-to-day. And it was precisely that identity, that sense of sharing something old and familiar that belonged to no one but us, that sense of exuberance in a common enterprise of struggle and survival, that made going to church something special, something that was more of an enjoyment than a duty. Even though we denied all that and told ourselves— sitting with our airs of middle class refinement and Sunday faces—that this new church experience was *our* kind of religion, we knew that something was missing.[18]

This rediscovery and reclaiming of tradition for Black RCA members is a by-product of the Black Council. This can be appreciated in a denomination that is still seen by many as a repository of Dutch-American roots. How then can these two traditions exist side-by-side with integrity without encountering each other's stark differences?

Even for some Blacks, though, this reawakening to the value of the Black religious tradition for their survival and well-being has not been easy to accept. To some, the separation from Black religious tradition was not a casual and superficial one, but a deep psychological break. Accompanying this separation was frequently an openness to religious fare quite foreign to that of their upbringing.

Analyzing this can be very difficult. Some who chose to explore religious life outside the Black church did so while

18   Wilmore, op. cit.

harboring a faulty understanding of institutionalized racism in churches. If they would just ignore race as a factor in human relations, perhaps it would go away. By abandoning their own cultural traditions, by changing their personal mannerisms and altering their physical appearance to suit the tastes of the dominant culture, some believed, they would cease to be the hate-objects of white bigots.

That racism infects the church is a blind spot for some Black people who have joined white congregations and denominations. To them, racism is non-existent in any situation where individual white people treat them cordially as individuals. This was the orientation of some at the first Black Caucus meeting. They opposed naming the organization the *Black* Council. They conceded that racism existed *in society*, but they considered the church to be categorically different. For they believed the church was a place of refuge from the problems of society and they resented the Black Council for bringing controversy into the one "free space" they felt they had.

Some Black people have felt that an open identification with the Council would jeopardize their relationship with their white pastor. In a few cases, they were right. Some have generally been involved less than others in church affairs, although quite active in community affairs. Still others have forthrightly opposed racism in church and society but, for their own reasons, have not been very involved in the Black Council *per se*. Each year, however, the number of those getting involved is increasing.

Overwhelmingly, those who have worked with the Council since its inception, as well as those who joined in later, are persons who play key roles in their local churches. In their local roles, they have learned the importance of being active in church affairs beyond their own congregations, since, in a presbyterial system, very important matters that affect the local situation are decided in higher judicatories.

Council members have come to terms with what it means for them to be Black Christians in a predominantly white denomination. Understanding this helped them render more effective and responsible service. They generally have good relations with whites on a personal level, and they are inclined to see their concern for racial justice as mainly an institutional concern, not as an issue of personality, focused upon individuals.

Persons active in Council work take seriously their involvement in the church, which emanates from their personal faith. They show great tolerance for the hard work it usually takes to find the answers to life's tough questions. More often than not, their church involvement is but an extension of their involvement in other facets of life. They tend to be activists who do not limit their concern for fair treatment and just relations to the ecclesiastical realm. Several have given exemplary leadership to secular groups seeking solutions to similar problems.

The founders of the Council expected to find allies among those whites who had been outspoken on the race issue before the Black Council was established. Yet, as time passed, it became evident that the interests of the two groups were not synonymous. In fact, some such whites have been among the Council's most outspoken opponents.

The creation of the Black Council in 1969 opened the way for other racial/minority groups to organize in the RCA. The "American Indians" organized themselves in 1970, followed by Hispanics in 1974 and Pacific-Asians in 1980. Each of these groups, while coming into existence under different circumstances, has expressed concern about issues of identity, Christian education, representation on policy bodies, leadership development, congregational development, and social justice. As time passed, the Councils developed good working relationships in those areas of shared concern, understanding that they also had some distinctive needs and priorities.

One example of their mutual concern was the election of a new General Secretary for the Reformed Church in 1983. The following is a communique that was sent by three of the Councils in April of that year:

Dear Committee Members:

We, the Executive Committees of the Black Council, Hispanic Council, the Council for Pacific and Asian American Ministries, meeting jointly on April 14, 1983 in Newark, New Jersey, wish to share with you the following concerns regarding the selection of a General Secretary for the Reformed Church in America.

We share our concern in the light of the Biblical mandate that each part of the body of Christ is to be committed to all other parts of that same body. We also note our church's commitment to diversity as articulated in the denominational priority "Crossing Cultural Barriers: Reaching Receiving in Christ."

It is our stated consensus that the person selected to be General Secretary must exhibit the following characteristics:

1. A demonstrated commitment to racial justice in both the United States and in other parts of the world;
2. A sensitivity to the needs and concerns of racial minority groups within the Reformed Church in America;
3. A willingness to work with the minority Councils in addressing racial justice issues and in bringing the gifts, perspectives and contributions of racial groups to the Reformed Church in America; and
4. An active commitment and sensitivity to the needs and concerns of women and for justice for women.

If none of the candidates currently being considered exhibit these characteristics, we urge the General Secretary Search Committee to take the additional time necessary to seek other more qualified candidates.

Also, we affirm the presence of Clara Woodson and Ella White on the Search Committee and stand with them as they attempt to include the above-stated characteristics as part of the overall criteria being used to select a General Secretary.

Sincerely,
(signed)
Earle N. S. Hall, Chair, Black Council
Johnny Alicea-Baez, Chair, Hispanic Council
Moody Yap, Chair, Pacific and Asian Council

As each of the other Councils came into being, some whites tried to spotlight how they differed from the Black Council. They were referred to as being "less militant" than the Black Council and more open to whites. The fact is, however, each of the groups went about representing their constituencies in the best possible manner and with integrity. They have rightly felt no obligation to try to imitate any other group in pursuing their objectives. At the same time, they have been quite astute at avoiding being used as a counter to the Black Council and have welcomed close cooperation with it. In 1974, when the Hispanic Council was petitioning the General Synod for formal recognition, it was proposed by the General Synod Executive Committee that the Black Council budget be cut by a third in order to fund the Hispanic Council. The Hispanic Council, led by Raymond Rivera, refused to accept funding if it were to come at the expense of the Black Council. This is just one of many illustrations of the spirit of solidarity that prevailed.

Black Council Priorities

Christian Education

In *Black People and the Reformed Church in America*, Noel Erskine wrote about a November 1971 conference on Black Christian Education (BCE) at Stony Point, New York, involving Millie Green and the Black Council. Ms. Green worked with Black and white RCA young people at that time but was trying to initiate a BCE program. Erskine pointed out that an agreement was reached at the Stony Point meeting regarding the importance of Black Christian Education as a distinct program, but he goes on to point out that a grant for this program was not forthcoming. Convincing the denomination of the significance of Black Christian Education was no small task for Ms. Green and her supporters. When the church's General Program Council finally voted $20,000 for the three-year effort, this was a far cry from the total program Green had conceived. But arriving at that amount resulted from determined negotiation, and John Buteyn, the then Secretary for World Mission, was quite instrumental in helping the recommending body reach an agreement.

Before the BCE Program could get started, it was fraught with problems. For one thing, many Black people were hard to convince that there was any such thing as *Black* Christian education. Those who were slow to believe felt that there was only one kind of Christian education and that was *Christian* education. This was easy to understand because of Black folks' strong conviction, rooted in their historical experience and belief, that the Christian faith was beyond race. However, what they would discover, as the conversation continued over several months, was that what they had always presumed to be simply "Christian" education was really Christian education from a certain perspective—the perspective of those who did not know the experience of Black people in America. On even

45

closer analysis, they could see that even church education materials produced *by Blacks* often did not directly reflect the Black experience. Instead, it often conveyed the cultural biases of affluent and middle-class values that were frequently alien to Black life.

Making the argument that God speaks to people in their own language and in their own situation was easy enough, so once a close look at the materials revealed the aforementioned biases, a few people became involved. That, however, was just the beginning. Even some of those who signed on early brought their skepticism with them. And given the fact that virtually all new materials would have to be developed by the participants, and because very few professionals had begun to try to meet this need, some of the pioneers were that much more reluctant.

The development of Black Christian Education in the Reformed Church in America was due largely to the determination, vision, and sheer salesmanship of Millie Green. Sometimes, when the going got rough, the program was kept alive only by the force of her personality and the loyalty that her own enthusiasm engendered. More and more persons began to see the urgency of BCE in its own right and, as greater cooperation was spurred among people from other denominations who had begun to work along similar lines, this creative program got under way in earnest.

As ecumenical projects developed, it became evident that the RCA was more advanced in the field than some other denominations. This was most evident in the BCE Task Force of the Joint Education Development Program, started by six predominately white denominations, including the RCA. There, Ms. Green found she had already addressed many of the issues and had gained a greater degree of support for the program from her denomination than some of her colleagues had from theirs.

Green's legacy was her leadership in defining and conceptualizing Black Christian Education in such a way as to make BCE a lasting part of the Black Christian's vocabulary. "New Roads of Faith" was a popular filmstrip that characterized the best of the BCE Program's achievements, and it borrows much from her work. The Erskine book was inspired by her, and it became the church's Black members' contribution to the RCA's 350th Anniversary in 1978. Dr. Erskine addressed the General Synod that year at Columbia University.

Still, BCE did not take hold in the way Millie Green expected. If one agreed that the customary church-school material was essentially white in its orientation, how could it be retained? Black Christian Education was an indictment of existing church education programs in Black churches, and the two approaches could not exist without the sponsoring church contradicting itself. Only a few churches dared to see this and to face up to it.

In too many cases, BCE remained simply the special interest of a few highly motivated people in the congregation who worked at it without challenging their church's old education program. Sometimes the Sunday school had entrenched leadership that lacked educational skills, innovative abilities, or even dedication to the students. So BCE advocates often sidestepped these problems and took on BCE as an alternative. This may be why the program was never institutionalized by churches and why, after all that was done to promote it, churches still had a weak commitment to it.

As indicated earlier, BCE was only part of Green's job; she also had some responsibility for denominational youth work. While she always demonstrated commitment to Black youth by ensuring their participation in the larger RCA youth programs, her involvement with BCE gave her work with youth an additional dimension.

47

She became more insistent and less compromising about Black youth agendas and about the function of the leaders of youth. She insisted that, if Black youth were to take part in the larger church's youth programming, activities had to have programs that appealed specifically to Black youth. Previously, programs had been designed without concern for what might interest Black youth. When challenged, white staff were usually willing to make some adjustments in order to accommodate them, but not to alter the program in any fundamental way.

This was, after all, the era of "integration." If Black people wanted to participate, they were welcome, but the true test of whether they "belonged" was whether they could fit into the established program. In many ways, the RCA still was an ethnic church in those regions of the nation where the church was strongest. So the idea of designing a program to suit a different group was a novel and unsettling idea. The operating assumption seemed to be that whatever whites planned for themselves would be good enough for everyone else, so Blacks should try to fit in if they could. This was never explicitly stated as a reason for the reluctance to fully accommodate Green's ideas. "Lack of funds" was usually the reason given.

Green's advocacy for more relevant youth programs for Blacks went on for some time. Her white colleagues usually made concessions and agreed to alter planned programs in order to reflect their sensitivity to the concerns she raised, but this way of doing things had its limits, as had become obvious by 1974, when, with staff support from Green and the Black Council, Brian Walker, a youth member of the Black Council from Brooklyn's New Lots Reformed Church, was invited to address the General Synod regarding "Third World youth" participation at the RCA-sponsored "International Youth Gathering," scheduled for August that year in Toronto, Canada. The following resolution was read by Walker and adopted by the Synod:

> Realizing the richness of Third World cultures, we wish to share our life experiences with the youth of the world. Such endeavors in the past to bring together diverse cultural background have met with dismal failure. Instead of representing the Third World in a meaningful way, such youth functions have been homogeneous in their make-up.

To alleviate this problem, be it resolved that the Reformed Church in America:

- Include Third World persons on the planning boards and staff, if possible, of future national, regional and local youth functions;
- Make a commitment to recruit more Third World youth to attend these functions;
- Call upon the Black, Hispanic and American Indian Councils to aid in the recruiting of these peoples;
- Use its resources to provide financial support to individual Third World youth who may be financially hard pressed to attend such functions; and
- To prevail upon the General Synod to use its power and/or influence to reserve the 100 Third World slots in question for the meeting in Toronto.

The conditions that may have made the participation of Black youth meaningful were not met, because a number of them who had been active in the effort to put these concerns before the Synod did not attend the Toronto meeting. Instead, with the help of Green, they held a separate "Third World Youth Gathering."

Green's role in the boycott of the "International Youth Gathering" and in organizing an alternative conference marked the beginning of her alienation from her white colleagues. By then, she had developed a strong identification with Africa and would soon change her name to Faraja Araba Nkroma. Her sense of vocation and the expectations that the RCA had of her increasingly conflicted. It was just a matter of time before she would leave the RCA. In 1977, she moved to Tanzania, East Africa, where she lived for the next 8 years.

The work that Faraja Nkroma began in Black Christian Education was continued by her successor, Edwina "Wyn" Wright. Nkroma's contribution was to define and to advocate BCE. Wyn Wright's contribution was to strengthen its programmatic implementation. Using the basic design that Nkroma had developed, Wyn developed a strategy that took into account the needs of the churches and the limited resources with which she had to work. She assisted advocates in congregations across the denomination in developing their skills for church education. With this training, they began implementing BCE at the local level. They were enabled to organize a program in their own church, and to become consultants to other churches interested in starting their own programs. Wyn recognized that she could not develop individual programs in individual churches, acting alone.

Thusly, "BCE Consultants" were mobilized and they continued their work even after Wright left her position two years later to continue her formal theological studies.

Advocacy for BCE, however, was never quite as persistent or aggressive as it had been before Nkroma left, and after each change in its staff leadership the program suffered a little. Wright, for example, was given staff responsibilities that did not allow her to concentrate fully on BCE as Nkroma had. When Wright left the staff, the program was directed, in cooperation with consultants across the country, by Dr. Wilbur Washington. Dr. Washington worked part-time until funding was completely eliminated during the denomination's budget crisis in 1981.

By the early 1980s, after the era of the International Youth Gathering and the BCE Program, denominational commitment to Christian Education began waning. Recently, however, a national youth emphasis has gotten underway again, as has a Council on Christian Education. Time will tell whether the concerns that Blacks expressed in those two areas in the past will be adequately addressed in these latest undertakings.

Black youth's need to have some significant involvement in the life of their denomination today is no less important than it was when Walker addressed the General Synod in 1974. Furthermore, after having experienced the impact that BCE has had on the faith of Black RCA members, it is hard to imagine how these members will carry on without it.

Black Christian Education was one of the early priorities of the Black Council. Now that the progress of this program has stalled, the Council will need to consider strategies for putting it back on the denomination's agenda.

RCA Policy Bodies

As was shown earlier, in its final report to the General Synod in 1969, the Commission on Race saw the importance of Black people serving on denominational policy and program bodies. Participation by Blacks in policy formulation and program development was also affirmed that year in the *Response to the Black Manifesto*. The General Program Council was the first of these bodies to make allowance for Black Council representation in its constitution. The General Synod Executive Committee came later. Black Council participation there was permitted by an exceptional arrangement, so such participation was not guaranteed. B. Moses James became the first Black person to serve on the General Synod Executive Committee when Norman Vincent Peale, pastor of the historic Marble Collegiate Church in New York City, serving on the Committee as Past-President of the General Synod, resigned to make it possible.

Prior to 1969, the names of some Black persons appeared among the lists of members of policy and advisory bodies. This is true of the Christian Action Commission and the now defunct Board of North American Missions, for example. Earlier on, two Black persons had served on the Commission on Race. Continuous Black involvement in these entities, however, was not assured. When a Black committee member's term expired on any given church body, a long time could pass before another Black person might be appointed or elected. Even then, it was not expected that these persons would represent the concerns of the church's Black members.

When the Black Council spoke of representation, it had in mind representation that would focus attention upon the challenges and interests of the Black community as a whole. Representation was necessary for the whole church to take full advantage of Black people's presence in the church. It was not presumed that Blacks would have a single perspective on matters but rather that, by representing their own experiences, they would bring different insights to bear on issues that came under consideration.

Involvement by Blacks, and later by other racial minority groups, was considered important by all. The question remaining was, how was this to be achieved? Year after year, the Council appealed to the judicatories to "do all they could" to see that a Black person was elected to represent them on one policy body or another. Some did. But, for the most part, Black participation on bodies of the General Synod was sporadic at best. This was frustrating to the Council. It smacked of bad faith. The highest policy-making body of the church had expressed its support for Black participation. Yet, the "lesser" judicatories were doing little or nothing to carry out this decision.

This did not change until 1979, ten years after the issue was first stated as a denominational goal. Coming to the realization that it was unlikely that Blacks would have consistent participation on RCA policy bodies if the "normal procedures" were the sole means employed to elect them, the Joint Committee on the Relationships and Responsibilities of Minority Councils and Denominational Policy Bodies recommended an Affirmative Action Plan that would ensure Black participation on all policy bodies that the Councils considered important to their work. This plan did not come easily. It took hours of sometimes heated negotiation in session after session.

One of the subjects that weighed heavily in the discussion was how an Affirmative Action plan might affect the approach to representation in presbyterial church polity. The advocates of Black participation were very cognizant of this issue and respectful of it. However, they felt strongly that preserving polity should not have priority over including people in the decision-making process that had been historically excluded because of race. The adopted plan was designed to strike a balance between the integrity of the system and ensuring representation for previously marginalized groups.

After the adoption of the plan, Black participation and that of other non-European peoples increased noticeably. Blacks began serving on the Board of Theological Education, the Theological Commission, the Historical Commission, the Commission on Christian Unity, the Christian Action Commission, the General Synod Executive Committee, the General Program Council, and the Nominations Committee. Some were named by their judicatories and some were appointed by their respective Councils. But participation by Blacks and other people of color on the policy bodies of the entire church was now institutionalized. The Black Council stressed the importance of Black members of these bodies being acquainted with the interests of the larger community of Black RCA members and that they be regular attendees at the annual Black Caucus.

Leadership Development for Clergy and the Laity

Throughout the late 1950s and the early-to-mid 1960s, when the RCA was addressing racial justice issues at General Synod meetings and when the Synod was becoming more and more aware of the challenges involved with Black persons joining the RCA in larger numbers, the absence of Black voices from many of the discussions on these issues was evident. This is not to say that Black people lacked concern about the issues that were on the agenda, but Blacks played virtually no visible role in national church life on those occasions when they could have made their voices heard.

The absence of a Black perspective in national church affairs was evident before Black leadership began speaking out, and the urgency of developing Black leadership helped set the agenda of the Council in its earliest days. Too few Black persons were knowledgeable of the basics of how the national and regional church functioned. The *Book of Church Order* and other governance documents that guided denominational procedures were yet unfamiliar to many prominent members of local congregations. How could elders and deacons fulfill their leadership responsibilities without more training? In some cases, in some churches, important decisions were being made that lay people did not fully comprehend. They sometimes failed to ask questions or to insist on answers. Actions were sometimes taken without their appropriate participation because of the vacuum of ignorance that existed. The potential consequences of this were staggering, and it had to stop if predominantly Black congregations were to be viable and self-governing.

The situation of Black pastors was not much different from that of the laity. As of 1982, only three of the more than twenty Black RCA ministers that served in the denomination had even been part of the denomination ten years earlier. This meant that, in the early 1980s, 85% of Black RCA ministers were relatively new. In 1972, there were no Black students enrolled in RCA seminaries. Rev. Samuel Williams was the only Black pastor who had come up through the ranks. He graduated from the RCA-supported Southern Normal School in Brewton, Alabama; then from Central College in Pella, Iowa; and then from Western Theological Seminary in Holland, Michigan. The only other pastor who came close to such a long-tenured affiliation was Dr. Wilbur Washington. His first contact with the RCA came when he enrolled in New Brunswick Theological Seminary in New Jersey. Previously, he had been a member of the African Methodist Episcopal Church.

Not only had there been far fewer Black pastors in the denomination a decade before, but Black members of the church had not yet begun to express a preference for Black pastoral leadership. Blacks did not yet feel at home and did not feel free to make demands. Some of the early Black members acknowledged later that they sometimes thought about having a Black minister, but never made of point of pursuing this because they assumed that none were available.

Close bonds of friendship sometimes developed between these new Black members and their white pastors. Whenever interest in having a Black pastor was expressed in a way that was threatening to the incumbent pastor, some Black members found it hard to separate their personal feelings for the pastor from their concerns for the congregation. Personal fear of job-loss and of rejection were often couched in theological terms. "The Christian community knows no race" was a frequently used argument against considering the need for Black pastoral leadership.

Congregations were often not able to freely discuss whether having a Black pastor might lead to growth and progress, for fear of being accused of being Black racists (a fear that was not unfounded). The idea that an open, honest discussion of this issue might have led to the conclusion that, in some cases, the church would be better off with a white pastor did not seem to occur to people resisting such open discussion.

The Black Council never opposed the right of predominantly Black congregations to call a white pastor. However, the Council advocated churches having the *option* of calling a Black pastor. And it was maintained that the decision to call *any* pastor should be based on a full assessment of every aspect of the church's needs. The racial composition of the congregation and the community in which it is located must be considered in this equation. The paradox of this situation is that those who have resisted a "Black pastor for Black congregations" approach have said nothing in opposition to the fact that no Black RCA pastor leads a congregation that is predominantly white.

The fact that having a Black pastor has not long seemed to be an option for Black RCA members may have been detrimental to some congregations. In its report to the General Synod in 1977, The Council suggested that numerical growth and financial giving are linked to the presence of Black pastoral leadership in some congregations. More than the quantifiable assets that often accompany competent Black pastors, value must also be associated with pastoral care and the implicit knowledge of the tradition that comes with being Black. Quality pastoral care is greatly dependent upon a profound understanding of the social, cultural, and psychological context in which the parishioner is living. There is sound evidence that one can do little to assist a person in crisis if one lacks this basic understanding.

Presumably, there are white persons who can provide suitable pastoral care to Blacks. And merely being Black does not automatically qualify a Black person for this responsibility. But, overall, it is much more likely that Black pastors will be better equipped than their white counterparts, for reasons that go far beyond individual intent, dedication, or training.

As noted earlier, the very role of the Black pastor in the Black community is historically different, in some fundamental ways, than that of the white pastor's role in the white community. The institutional church in the two communities also serves different functions. The Black church remains more central in the wide range of issues arising among Black persons and in Black people's struggle to survive. The Black church is more important in the politics, economics, education, and social life of Black people that the white church is to white people. Whites have built different institutions to meet their different needs, and the white church consequently has become more specialized and limited to "spiritual" matters. Pastors of Black people must grasp this distinction between Black and white approaches to "church," not just from the standpoint of being sympathetic to it, but understanding it as a matter of life and death. Appreciating the unique aspects of Black Christian tradition is essential to understanding the Black Council's promotion of Black pastoral leadership.

Perhaps the most controversial development involving a white pastor and the Black Council occurred in the case of a white pastor in East Harlem. The pastor had been an early advocate for Black people in the period following the 1950s. He was honored and respected by many for his efforts to discourage the RCA congregations, losing members to the suburbs, from "abandoning the city." He was elevated to high positions of leadership partly because of this stance and as a sign that the larger church was determined to heed his appeal. However, as it turned out, he was not a strong supporter of the Black Council. And when he chose to resign as pastor of his largely Black and Hispanic congregation after nearly two decades of service, he insinuated that the Council had been responsible for pushing him out. This pastor was generally quite popular among his members and the Council would have had no leverage to pressure his resignation, nor would it have had a motive. Nevertheless, this became a rumor that spread to different quarters in the denomination, and it became an eye-opening revelation to his Black admirers. A pastor who had been a pioneer in sensitizing his church to racial issues had become a symbol of opposition to Black self-determination.

The coming of Black preachers to the denomination was a new reality. Because most of them came from non-presbyterial denominations, their special needs demanded attention. Their educational backgrounds varied greatly, and their effectiveness had to be enhanced through targeted continuing education. The fact that most of them were serving in churches that were experiencing some kind of crisis made their effective service that much more urgent.

These needs were uppermost in the minds of a group of about eight ministers when they visited New Brunswick Theological Seminary, the oldest continuing Protestant seminary in the USA and the RCA's first seminary. Dr. Howard Hageman, a respected author and pastor, was in the early days of his tenure as Seminary President and the visiting pastors sought to explore with him how the seminary could help meet the needs of the newly emerging Black clergy.

From that time onwards, New Brunswick began to make strides in increasing Black student enrollment. It brought on board a full-time Black member of the faculty and it developed an experimental program intended to meet the educational needs of urban pastors. The full-time faculty post was reduced to a part-time position in the wake of the seminary's financial crisis in the early 1980s. Under President Hageman, however, the envisioned collaboration between the seminary and the visiting clergy never came to fruition. The particular needs of Black congregations were never fully the focus of the seminary's attempt at innovative programming. Rev. Robert White, Dr. Hageman's successor, held out hope for closer cooperation.

In looking to the denominational seminaries to be responsive to the concerns of the denomination's Black members, it is not suggested that the RCA seminaries have no responsibility to provide theological education to non-RCA students. Nevertheless, given the acute challenges facing RCA members, and given the RCA's limited experience with Black people, the seminaries' innovative involvement with Blacks in general should start with those in their own denomination. The Black Council has focused its expectation for relevant theological education on New Brunswick, probably because of its proximity to the highest density of Black RCA members. Western, like New Brunswick, once had at least one full-time Black faculty member, although its Black enrollment, as of this writing, has remained relatively smaller or non-existent.

What is needed are courses in church government, focused particularly on its practical use to accomplish church goals in an orderly manner; courses in Reformed theology; so too are courses in RCA church history, specifically aimed at acquainting Black pastors and lay leaders with the historical roots of the denomination. Such courses may require some adjustment in the way the seminary organizes its program and how it utilizes its faculty, but meeting these needs is crucial for the institutions. This can be done without compromising academic standards.

Recognizing leadership development to be the urgent challenge of the future as far as the Black members were concerned, the General Program Council agreed to fund a program in Black leadership development in 1974, as part of its Urban Mission Advance. Funds from this program have gone to help lay people and ministers.

An annual meeting of Black RCA ministers has made it possible for this group to discuss challenges they confront in areas of service where they are sometimes pioneers. They are frequently the only Black pastors in their judicatories and, in spite of the best efforts of their white brethren, they may not always enjoy sufficient support from their colleagues.

The annual meeting of pastors provided a sense of community. It has also fostered consultation and mutual support among them between meetings. In addition to the personal support they experience, their deliberations usually help clarify problems they face as a group. The pastors' operational definition of self-reliance and their concern about ministries of churches in racial transition are two examples of issues that have emerged in these meetings.

The yearly B. Moses James Colloquium on Black Religion is part of a leadership development process. It is named in honor of that Rev. James who was the first chairperson of the Council. He died in 1975, just days before completing his second full term.

The first two James Colloquia were held at New Brunswick and Western Seminaries, respectively. In later years, they were held either during the ministers Conference or during the annual Black Caucus meetings. The lectures delivered at these colloquia have been widely circulated to RCA members and to interested persons in other denominations. Lecturers at this annual event included such notables as Gayraud S. Wilmore, James Cone, Lawrence N. Jones, Noel Erskine, Burgess Carr, Charles Sherrod, Howard Dodson, Lawrence E. Carter, Barbara Williams Skinner, Cornel West, Wyatt T. Walker, Dr. Robert Johnson, and Ivan Van Sertima. The intent of the James Colloquium is to keep alive the rich religious heritage of Black people as well as to draw attention to the emerging themes that are being explored by scholars and activists.

In all the leadership development programs that the Council has organized, the needs of the laity have been a priority. In the first round of activity just after the leadership program was funded, workshops were conducted that were specifically aimed at lay people. In these workshops, the subjects being considered included parliamentary procedure, Consistory training, note-taking, record-keeping, and group dynamics.

The largest group of Black people gather each year in the Black Caucus. Hence, this forum has provided excellent opportunities for leadership development activities. This has been especially true of workshops and seminars on urgent social issues, such as concern about the family and racism in the media and in children's books. How to handle such important church business as calling and evaluating ministers has also been the subject of training sessions.

A wide range of presentations have been made at Black Caucus meetings as part of this leadership development program. Guest presenters have included such speakers as noted historian Lerone Bennett, Jr.; John E. Jacob, president of the National Urban League; Marian Wright Edelman, President of the Children's Defense Fund; South African theologian Allan

Boesak; Nobel Laureate Archbishop Desmond Tutu; noted television journalist Gil Noble; and many others.

In the early 1970s, the General Program Council instituted a scholarship fund for racial minority students. Initially, this fund was used as a matching grant for students attending RCA-related colleges. If a college were willing to offer a grant to a Black student, the denomination would offer a matching amount up to $1,500. By the mid-seventies, though, new criteria for using the funds were established. If a student were a member of an RCA congregation, that student could attend any institution of higher learning and be eligible for assistance. However, attending an RCA-related institution was necessary for those recipients who happened not to be members of a congregation affiliated with the denomination. Awards are based on need and on availability of funds. Over seventy Black students were assisted in the initial years of this program in the pursuit of college or seminary degrees.

Later in the seventies, the GPC stressed that leadership development for racial minority group members must be a continuing priority for the denomination on a national level. Much still needed to be done. However, because of the RCA's intentional support for leadership training among Blacks, lay people were much more informed about their adopted church and they were much more engaged in denominational affairs. They were more equipped to function at the local level because of their increased awareness of the basic rules by which the church's business is done.

Self-Reliance Is a Pressing Matter

Most RCA congregations located in predominantly Black communities were dependent on church bodies beyond their local congregation to help pay their basic expenses. This gradually changed, though, as churches saw that self-reliance was linked to their sense of dignity and to their self-determination. Increasingly, they found it humiliating to make requests for funds that required them to justify their needs.

The dependence of Black congregations had begun, as noted earlier, during the process of racial transition in local congregations and neighborhoods. In order to keep the doors open (and some churches failed at this), appeals for financial support had to be made to "friends" from outside the immediate worshipping community. The strongest financial members of the churches had left for the suburbs and the newcomers were either not as financially able to carry the load as their predecessors or were too few in number or had yet to develop a sense of responsibility for what was, to them, still a "foreign" church.

Dependency, however, continued long after the transition period. White pastors of these churches, with varying degrees of success, were able to cultivate financial backers for their work among Black people much like missionaries to foreign lands. White pastors in Black communities were sometimes regarded as "domestic missionaries." This helps explain what some meant by the term "urban missions."

While this paradigm of dependence was evolving in the churches, most Black members did not know what was going on. They saw themselves simply as regular church members, not as objects of mission. They were often unaware of the details of the church's finances, which was fine with them in many cases, since they were not being pressured to give more in the offering plate, as they had been in the churches they had left. They were also not being encouraged to sponsor fund-raising events, so they were satisfied to leave all that behind. In fact, this was an attractive feature that many of them used to persuade their friends to come to the new church with them. Also, don't forget the appeal of the short sermon!

Longtime Black members of consistories claimed not to have been fully informed about church business, yet they should have known that the money was coming from somewhere! There are churches that still balance their budgets with gifts from "friends." Originally, this was a way of keeping the churches afloat at a time of particular difficulty, but it deteriorated into a pattern of long-term dependence that severely thwarted the development of the Black members' sense of belonging and ownership in the RCA family.

The impairment caused by such dependence sometimes came like a sudden jolt, as when lay leaders discovered, after calling a Black pastor, that funds they had received from financially wealthy congregations for a number of years were earmarked not for the ministry, but for the previous pastor. The fact that such funds might have disappeared or dramatically declined with the coming of a Black pastor was a rude awakening for Black Consistory members.

Some members responded by working harder to increase the level of support coming from the congregation. Still others took this as justification for their reluctance to call a Black minister in the first place. Simply put, this latter group rather enjoyed the fact that white pastors had sufficient connections in the denomination to attract dollars to their church. They appeared not to care about the negative repercussions of this attitude on the future of the local ministry.

Black congregations were not alone in receiving aid from sources outside the local church, but their subsidization was a bit different from that of dependent white congregations. The Black congregation had not yet found its place as an ordinary part of the RCA. The RCA had not anticipated the emergence of predominantly Black congregations, hence, the larger church's responsibility to these churches was not appropriately understood. In addition, some whites assumed that Blacks were unable or unwilling to carry their own share of the responsibility. It is the same stereotype of Black people that has been fostered by the federal and state welfare system. Never mind that most people receiving welfare assistance are white; the image of welfare that is projected throughout society is of a program that benefits mostly racial minorities.

In any event, Black people were slow to shoulder the responsibility of supporting churches they had inherited from fleeing whites. This helped reinforce the stereotype. This stereotype is at the heart of why it is so important for Black people to achieve self-reliance in the churches. The process of racial reconciliation will be derailed if Blacks are perceived not only by whites but even by themselves as always being on the receiving end.

Mutual responsibility and reciprocity are not something that is restricted to the RCA; nor is it limited to churches in the USA. Self-reliance is also one of the main preoccupations of churches in the Third World. In Africa, this issue was once called "Moratorium." African church leaders appealed to churches in Western countries not to send more missionaries until the church of that continent could assess its own needs. What was and still is at issue in Africa and in so many other areas of the developing world is the very selfhood and integrity of the church.

Another example of this is the "Three Self Movement" among churches in China. Churches there want to be self-administering, self-supporting, and self-propagating; and their motivation, although rooted in different historical circumstances, is akin to the Black Council's desire for the predominantly Black congregations to be self-reliant. Formerly oppressed or dependent groups in churches all over the world are saying, in effect, "If we are to be reconciled in Christ, then we must stop behaving as if we were the wards of those who should be our sisters and brothers."

When the voices in favor of self-reliance and self-determination are raised, a countervailing voice comes from agents of old-style mission. That voice reminds us that the church of Christ is universal. It says that those who promote selfhood for the church in one area are denying foreign missionaries a role, and thus are denying the church's universality. This is symptomatic of the arrogance that permeated the Western missionary movement. After all the years they have been promoting their own nationalistic and ethnocentric brand of faith, and after all the damage they have done by exporting cultural imperialism and colonial domination, they still have not come to accept that their missionary activities are sometimes more harmful than helpful.

Lest the foregoing comments about churches abroad be understood only in terms of international church relations, it should be said that much of the same challenge and much of the same resistance as we see in the international arena obtains within the RCA and within other denominations. Some try hard to discourage self-reliance as a goal because they fear the implications of a Black constituency that is a full partner in the denomination. They fear what new issues may be placed on the church's agenda and what new mission priorities may be proposed.

However, for the sake of true reconciliation and unity, Black RCA members must persevere in their commitment to self-reliance. Black church members must go beyond a rhetorical statement of commitment to self-reliance and do the hard work of mobilizing the churches and the individual members to achieve it. If, after examining this goal in a sincere and rational manner, achieving self-reliance seems not to be within the capacity of a given congregation for the foreseeable future, that church should consider the hard choice of merging with one or more RCA congregations in the vicinity. This latter option will not be considered by some churches that ought to choose it, because it is clearly not the most attractive one—especially for the congregation that wants to preserve its separate identity. Experience suggests, however, that a stigma attaches to a church, either from outside or from within, when it is dependent on others for as far into the future as one can see.

In Consistory meetings of such churches, little time is spent discussing ministry to human needs. Instead, virtually all their energy is devoted to solving financial problems. When the Black Caucus focused on self-reliance in 1974, it recognized that more concrete explanations would be needed to make it possible to operationalize the concept. The Black Ministers Conference developed a pragmatic definition that was subsequently affirmed by the Council and the Caucus. It explained that churches needed funding for three types of activities:

1. Capital improvements and mortgages for the church's physical plant;
2. Outreach programs that benefit the community in which the church is located and other mission-oriented undertakings; and
3. Ongoing expenses of the church, such as staff salaries, utilities, and minor building repair and maintenance. According to the ministers' definition, a church that covers the latter category from its own resources can be regarded as a self-reliant church.

They said further that, if supporters from outside the congregation contributed to community projects that are identified with the church, the host church must initiate such projects using its own resources. This is to underscore that the friendly assistance from partners from other communities would come at the invitation of churches with the community to be served. The emphasis would be on partnership, not paternalism.

By saying that those expenses in category no. 3 represented the minimum of self-reliance, the Ministers Conference did not mean to suggest that congregations shared no responsibility for mortgages and major capital improvements. If the church is capable of paying all of its expenses, including sending funds to support the denomination's benevolence budget, this is strongly urged. But if this is not possible, and if a church must prioritize because of its limited resources, they can be helped in this by the order of the three categories. If they pay their ongoing expenses, though, they are self-reliant by the accepted definition. If outside support for projects is withdrawn, the congregation's existence as a worshipping community is not jeopardized.

Mortgages and other major improvements are not considered an essential responsibility for the self-reliant congregation because the property of the church is held by the Classis, not by the congregation. Since Blacks have been subject to "urban removal" schemes historically, they do not assume for certain that they will remain in a given location over a long period of time. The churches in the area would remain a part of the RCA and its judicatories. When Blacks move away, they show little denominational loyalty to the RCA.

The Council's emphasis on self-reliance began at a time when some judicatories had begun to place tighter restrictions on the funds they could make available to churches. These restrictions, which were imposed because of budget constraints, make more apparent the practical value of self-reliance to the viability of congregations. When these restrictions were announced, some Black church leaders panicked because they knew what dramatic pressures this would bring to bear on their already precarious financial predicament. Some surmised that these restrictions were a punitive backlash against the Council's advocacy of self-reliance. Eventually, albeit in hindsight, most of them saw the restriction as a golden opportunity to pursue self-reliance more resolutely. The evidence of this determination is reflected in the several churches that reached or had concrete plans to reach this goal.

If Black congregations are to have a long-term future in the RCA, self-reliance must be applauded and encouraged, not feared or held in suspicion. Judicatories that provide assistance to churches in need know how fragile the situation of these churches is. If those churches that have a chance of survival are to become self-reliant, they will need help from agencies that have worked with them in the past. Self-reliance must be a joint effort of the congregation, the Classis, and the Particular Synod. The ability of the congregation to increase its own giving must be pursued in relation to the judicatory's plan to decrease aid. Should a judicatory decide to withdraw aid without an adequate process of negotiation with dependent congregations, this is likely to be an untenable burden to the congregation.

Some question whether self-reliance is possible for all churches. They say that some congregations will never be able to pay even their basic operating expenses. To confirm this view, they point to the low-income levels of the people and the high costs involved. While conceding that this may appear true in some situations, in all too many cases these churches suffer from long-standing patterns of low expectation fostered by paternalistic white pastors and from their inability to attract new members to help build their capacity. Admittedly, large numbers do not a faithful church make, but there is a limit to what a small group of persons can do to support a ministry. This must be taken into account, just as the inability of a church's leadership to attract new congregants should be considered in evaluating a church's potential. Numbers of new congregants may not be the all-important factor in such an evaluation, but it is a factor that cannot be ignored.

If a church cannot support itself, it should not be sustained with money from outside the community. By accepting the arguments advanced by those who advocate no-end-in-sight grants to these churches, one creates obstacles to developing mutual respect among people historically alienated by race and tradition.

This is a view of church development that will not come easy after two or more decades of dependence, and it is one that requires leadership from church judicatories. If they are to help, judicatories must urge leaders in congregations not to take on expenses they cannot afford; they must help keep self-reliance before congregations as an attractive option; and they must not avoid the difficult responsibility of engaging the local church in open dialogue about their future if their contribution as a distinct congregation appears to be in jeopardy.

When the General Program Council adopted its policy on Urban Ministry in 1978, the self-reliance theme was key. It was the Black Council's hope that the Policy Statement would stress the importance of empowering local churches as the locus of ministry by the RCA in Black inner-city communities. Implied in their position is a lack of confidence in extra-congregational ministries that are ostensibly intended to meet community needs, but that are not initiated or controlled by the nearest local RCA congregations. It is the local congregation's image and credibility that can rise or fall with the reputation of such extra-congregational projects, so their involvement with and custody of those projects is essential.

A more extensive discussion of the urban ministry policy will be taken up later.

South Africa

Because of the common theological and ecclesiastical roots that the RCA shares with the Dutch Reformed Church in South Africa, and given the seminal role of the latter in the creation of South Africa's racist apartheid system, potential Black members of the denomination were anxious to know what relationship, if any, existed between the American and the South African churches. And more importantly, they wanted to know the RCA's own position on apartheid. This is the question with which Black RCA members were confronted when they would inform other Black people of their own church affiliation. For several reasons, the issue of apartheid was not a casual one for the RCA. For a decade before the Black Council was established, the RCA had been corresponding with the South African church, expressing its objection to that church's support for apartheid policies. However, according to Dr. Marion DeVelder, General Secretary Emeritus of the RCA, this correspondence had little effect.

In 1967, The Christian Action Commission of the RCA proposed, and the General Synod adopted, the denomination's most comprehensive statement up to that time condemning apartheid.[19] The statement said, in part:

> The non-white is refused his essential humanity and dignity as he endures the 'pass laws', the compounds, the denial of a voice in his own affairs, the right of free speech, of assembly, of the right of petition, for redress of grievances. Arrest without charge and imprisonment without trial is a common occurrence. Because of its kinship with the Reformed Churches in South Africa, because of its concern for all people, white and non-white, the Reformed Church in

---

19 *Minutes of the General Synod,* 1967 (Christian Action Commission Report).

America continues to appeal to the consciences of the Christians of South Africa, calling upon them to reverse the patterns of racism and injustice.

This message was conveyed to the white Reformed churches in South Africa by DeVelder, as directed by the Synod that year. The following year, the South Africans responded in a way that indicated the seriousness with which they took the RCA statement.

A Plea for Understanding: A Reply to the Reformed Church in America was published in 1968 over the name of W. A. Landman of Cape Town, South Africa. This 144-page document may be accurately described as an *apologia* for South Africa's racist policies; its premise being that, if the RCA only had more accurate and updated information about what was actually going on in South Africa and about why the whites considered apartheid the only sensible way to organize South African society, they would not have issued their 1967 statement. The argument, essentially, was that such an understanding of the South African situation should be the basis of a dialogue between the Reformed Churches in the two countries.

When presented with this argument, the General Synod affirmed the principle of dialogue. An Ad Hoc Committee on South Africa was established in 1968 to determine how the denomination could best pursue contacts with the South African church. The first report of the Ad Hoc Committee was presented to the General Synod in 1969 by Raymond Pontier. All indications are that the RCA considered that its responsibility in South Africa was to dialogue with white Christians. They seemed to believe that if change was to come, it would come mainly by decision of the white Dutch Reformed Church members. They gave no apparent credence to the role of Black resistance. Because dialogue with the South Africans was considered inter-church contact, the responsibility for dialogue between the RCA and the white South African churches was placed in the hands of what was known at the time as the Commission on Christian Unity. The Ad Hoc Committee on South Africa continued for several years, and its stated primary concern was racial justice. Yet there is no indication that the denomination looked to its Black members to assist in guiding its actions. The RCA confessed to its South African partners-in-dialogue that the USA was not perfect in its treatment of non-white peoples. Despite this confession, the church kept ignoring the potentially valuable contribution Black RCA members might make on this issue, and it seemed unaware of the contradiction. Also, Black RCA members seemed just as complacent about making their voices heard. The one possible exception may be the participation of Dr. Wilbur Washington, a prominent pastor in the denomination and a graduate of New Brunswick Theological Seminary, in a discussion involving US and South African church leaders at a meeting of the World Alliance of Reformed Churches in Nairobi, Kenya in 1970.

The lack of Black involvement in determining the RCA's approach to apartheid South Africa, and the lack of contact on the part of the RCA with Black South African members of the Dutch Reformed Churches, made a difference in how the RCA behaved. The intransigence of white South Africans was not yet so evident to the world, and Blacks on both sides of the Atlantic had not begun to express themselves as they would later.

The Ad Hoc Committee on South Africa gave its first full report to the same General Synod meeting that called for the organization of the Black Council. Several years passed before the newly formed Black Council became meaningfully involved in the South Africa issue, but there was concern about South African's racist system from the Council's beginning.

This concern was demonstrated at a shareholder's meeting of Englehard Mines and Minerals Corporation, in which the RCA owned stock. The Council's executive director (this author) attended the meeting to protest that company's activities in South Africa. The RCA was the only member of the Interfaith Center on Corporate Responsibility (ICCR) that owned stock in this firm, from which it soon divested. Englehard, based in Newark, New Jersey, had become a wholly owned subsidiary of the Anglo-American Corporation, a South African mining conglomerate.

South Africa was a major focus of ICCR, an organization that enjoyed the strong personal support of Marion DeVelder, who, before his retirement as General Secretary of the RCA, served as chairperson of ICCR's Board of Directors. Much of the RCA's work against apartheid in the 1970s was in the area of corporate responsibility, but this drew relatively little attention. During that period, the Black Council's executive also represented the denomination on the ICCR Board, as did Marvin Hoff, then Secretary of Operations, who later became President of Western Theological Seminary.

The Council's executive director participated with DeVelder in one other important South Africa–related project: confronting International Business Machines (IBM) on the role of its computers in strengthening apartheid's military capability and in helping South Africa implement its draconian Pass Laws. DeVelder and Howard were part of a delegation that visited IBM's Chief Executive Officer at Armonk, New York, and they were participants in a hearing on the role of IBM in South Africa sponsored by ICCR at the Interchurch Center in New York. The proceedings of these hearings were published and widely distributed.

In 1973, the Black Caucus held its first formal discussion about South Africa. This discussion was one of several subject areas of interest from which Caucus delegates could choose. The resource person for the South Africa group was Victor Vockerodt, a young South African who had previously studied toward becoming a Roman Catholic priest. The response to this discussion was so strong that the Council began addressing the South Africa issue in more deliberate ways.

In 1974, South African theologian Dr. Allan Boesak visited the Office of the Black Council for the first time. Boesak was a Ph.D. candidate at Kampen in the Netherlands, and he was in the USA acquainting himself with the Black Theology movement. The significance of his contact with the Black Council would not become clear until years later, when Boesak returned to South African and immersed himself in the movement for freedom.

Informed by the students' growing radicalization in Cape Town and the rising expectations of the people in general, Boesak quickly emerged as one of the leading voices of progressive Christianity in South Africa. His dissertation, published under the title *A Farewell to Innocence,* became one of the most widely read statements of Black South African theology. It is an important book for understanding the theological underpinnings of apartheid and the struggle for its demise. In 1982, Boesak was elected president of the World Alliance of Reformed Churches at the same meeting where that organization suspended all the South African Dutch Reformed churches. Black Council member Dorothy James, the widow of B. Moses James, first Black Council chair, was an RCA delegate to this historic meeting.

During the year following Boesak's first visit to the Black Council office, more activities began to unfold that would bring Black Dutch Reformed Church members in South Africa into contact with Black members of the RCA. In October of 1975, Jan Luben Hoffman, a New Brunswick Seminary student, informed the Council (by telephone) that the Reverend Elia Tema, a Black pastor in the Black Dutch Reformed church in Orlando East in Soweto (Johannesburg), South Africa, had arrived to study in New Brunswick for that school year. This phone call helped launch a new chapter in the RCA's relationship with South Africa, in that it established a connection between the church and Black leadership of the Dutch Reformed churches for the first time.

Later in the week of that call, Rev. Tema made direct contact with the Black Council and arranged to attend its annual Black Caucus meeting a few days later at the Roosevelt Hotel in New York City.

It is uncanny how events unfolded. Tema had been invited to study at the seminary by President Howard Hageman; he was helped in his effort to make contact with Black people in the USA by a female white student; and when Tema arrived at the Caucus meeting, a film titled *The Last Grave at Dimbaza*, made illegally in South Africa, about the brutal repression of Blacks in that country, was being shown. Rev. Tema knew from experience the reality this film sought to convey, but it was the first time he had seen the film, since it could not be shown in South Africa. He was deeply moved and said that evening that although he was many miles away from his country, he felt very much at home.

For the rest of that school year, the Council continued cementing its relationship with Tema and becoming more acquainted with the church he represented. Tema was a leader in his denomination, and he had come to the USA with expectations of building ties with Black RCA members, and the RCA generally, on behalf of his sisters and brothers at home.

The Commission on Christian Unity, chaired by Dr. Charles Wissink of the New Brunswick faculty, also worked with Rev. Tema to cultivate interchurch relations. The dialogue with the

Ad Hoc Committee on South Africa had run its course. Rev. Tema provided a new opening. He helped to convince many during his stay that the future of South Africa was in the hands of those who resisted apartheid, not with those who were defending it.

By June of 1976, several things had happened that would impact the way the RCA related to South Africa. Rev. Tema visited RCA congregations in several parts of the county to tell the story of the people he represented. Many of his hosts were Black people, who were discovering how much they shared in common with Black South Africans in their struggle for liberation against racial oppression. Tema helped to lift up the issue of South Africa in the RCA's consciousness in a new way, because he engaged the church as a Black South African whom apartheid had sought to victimize. He challenged the church in the name of Christian faith to oppose South African apartheid more forcefully.

Previously, the RCA had dealt with white South Africans who attempted to show that apartheid was compatible with the Gospel. One exception, among others, was Beyers Naude, the banned white leader of the Dutch Reformed Church, who headed the Christian Institute. The RCA was one of the US churches that supported the Institute before it too was banned. Naude, after being banned for over five years, succeeded Bishop Desmond Tutu as General Secretary of the South African Council of Churches.

The RCA never accepted that the Gospel and apartheid were compatible, but Tema gave the denomination new energy and resolve to oppose the system it had denounced in 1967. Tema was a new element in a fifteen-year-old dialogue; so were the Black members of the RCA. Ironically, Elia Tema, and the natural sense of kinship he shared with the Black community in the RCA, did more to bring them into the South Africa debate and struggle than anything that had happened before that time.

In late 1975, the executive director of the Black Council attended the Fifth Assembly of the World Council of Churches (WCC) and in early 1976 became Moderator of the WCC's Programme to Combat Racism (PCR). The PCR was well known in South Africa and elsewhere for its support of southern Africa's liberation movements and this pulled the Black Council and the RCA even deeper into the South Africa issue.

The event that completely redefined the way RCA members came to look at South Africa, however, was the revolt by school children in Soweto on June 16, 1976. When the revolt began, the RCA General Synod was in session at Fairleigh Dickinson University in Madison, New Jersey, and the Reverend Sam Buti, Jr., the Secretary General of the Black Dutch Reformed Church in South Africa, had been invited to address the Synod meeting, at the urging of Rev. Tema. His presence at the Synod meeting at the precise time that the world's attention was focused upon the South African government's brutal repression of Black school children made quite an impact on the Synod delegates. This historic moment dashed all hope for dialogue with pro-apartheid South Africans.

When Tema returned to South Africa in the fall of 1977, he extended an invitation to the Black Council's representatives to come for a visit. The Council decided this visit should take place in conjunction with the Commission of Christian Unity because of the work the Commission had done in facilitating relations between the RCA and Tema's church. This joint venture, by two units of the General Synod, was the first illustration of the distinctive contribution that the Council could play in cultivating relations between the RCA and progressive South African Christians.

In its 1978 report to the General Synod, the Commission on

Christian Unity stated that "an invitation was received through the RCA Black Council for a Black RCA pastor to go to South Africa. The Black Council and the Commission on Christian Unity worked together on this matter....it does represent the best opportunity for the commission yet available and we pray such a visit will be realized in the near future."[20]

Understanding why this invitation was extended to the Black Council is important. After the Soweto riots in 1976, Black people who were identified with the pro-apartheid Dutch Reformed Church had credibility problems. The masses of people in South Africa tended to see the Black Dutch Reformed Church as too closely linked with the apartheid ideology, and it provides salary support for many pastors of Black congregations. To have white guests from the Reformed Church in America during that time would not have helped this credibility problem. While image was not the point of the Black Council visit, the fact that there were Black Americans who were *both* Reformed *and* actively opposed to apartheid would be all to the good.

White members of the denomination who opposed apartheid may not have understood the importance of the Council's role at first, but it became widely accepted that church actions regarding South Africa ought to be taken in consultation with the Black Council.

This has helped to clarify certain matters regarding the relationship that the whole church seeks to have with her Black members. The same challenge obtains with respect to the role of other people of color in the RCA too. The Hispanic Council, for example, has sometimes felt bypassed as the denomination sought to respond to the revolutionary movements in Central America.

---

20 *Minutes of the General Synod,* 1978, pp. 210-211.

Visas to South Africa were hard to come by, especially if one were suspected of being an opponent of that government's policy. Hence, the invitation that was extended by Tema and company in late 1977 was not honored immediately. Nevertheless, some highly visible events took place in 1978 to keep the region of southern Africa very much on the minds of church members.

In March of that year, Bishop Abel Muzorewa, a long-time opponent of white minority rule in Rhodesia, joined ranks with Ian Smith, the racist ex-prime minister. This resulted in what was referred to as the "Internal Settlement." The World Council of Churches had supported the Bishop's organization for several years prior to 1978. However, when, in August of 1978, the WCC awarded a grant to the Patriotic Front (a coalition of two movements still opposing Smith) but not to Muzorewa, a great controversy erupted. Some argued that the WCC had turned its back on a major religious leader; that it had not supported a genuine effort to avoid further bloodshed. Many critics expressed concern that the WCC was taking sides in a political conflict and some spoke openly against what they considered a demonstrated preference for movements that promoted Marxist solutions to the crisis. The Internal Settlement was known for its advocacy of Western-style capitalism. There were numerous charges against the Patriotic Front. It was accused of murder and general harassment of religious groups, though this was never substantiated.

During the time of the attack on the WCC, there were mixed responses from its member churches. Some understood that the Patriotic Front was the only outstanding opponent of "minority (i.e., white) rule"; that Muzorewa had, in effect, joined the ranks of his own oppressors. This seemed to affirm the WCC decision. Others openly questioned the organization's wisdom. The Salvation Army in Britain eventually withdrew from the WCC, even though the Salvation Army in Zimbabwe objected to their withdrawal. So did the Presbyterian Church of Northern Ireland.

Before stating its views, the RCA decided to evaluate the WCC's grant-making policies. Several units of the church were invited to appoint representatives to the committee to study this issue, but not the Black Council. The Council petitioned the General Synod Executive Committee to make room for Black Council participation. Rev. Donald Guest and Rev. Wilbur Washington served on this committee as a result. Overlooking the Council's interests was not uncommon in those days. The church still did not fully comprehend the Council's role beyond purely domestic, denominational issues. So, since it was more the rule than the exception that the Council was excluded from matters of obvious interest to the Black Council, albeit in another country, it was necessary to insist that its representatives be appointed to such study groups. This institutional inertia had to be confronted constantly. On top of this was the fact that, at the time, the Council's executive (this writer) was Moderator of the WCC's Commission for the Programme to Combat Racism, the grant sponsor, so he served as a consultant to the study committee.

The resulting report by the RCA was, in essence, support for the WCC action. However, the RCA was careful not to ignore the criticism that had been leveled against the WCC, even as it refused to join those who declared open season on the WCC's anti-racism program. To be sure, there were those who were disappointed in the RCA's position from both sides of the issue. Some felt it spoke too strongly and some felt it did not speak strongly enough. The General Synod voted that year, for example, that the RCA should not contribute to the PCR's Special Fund because it made "uncontrolled grants."

By February of 1979, visas to South Africa were approved

and Sara M. Smith, the Council's Chairperson, and the Reverend Earle N.S. Hall, its first vice-Chairperson, were off for a month-long visit to South Africa. As Black people living in the USA, theirs was a most unusual opportunity. They did not accept the "honorary white" status that was customarily assigned to Black visitors to South Africa, which would allow them to utilize public facilities and to have wide mobility in a way denied to Black South Africans. Furthermore, they went with the understanding that they would be allowed to stay in the homes of their Black hosts for the duration of their stay and would be able to travel wherever their hosts wanted to take them, without restriction. The cost of their travel was covered by a combination of support from the Black Ministers Conference, the Black Council, and the Commission on Christian Unity. There was no question that this visit was historic. It was a milestone in relations between the RCA and the Black Church in South Africa.

The visit was a phenomenal success by all standards, as was attested to by the Reverend Sam Buti, Jr. in 1981, when he was a speaker at the Black Caucus banquet. He recalled what it had meant for Smith and Hall to come and live with them and to worship with them as sister and brother. He also remembered Smith's having spoken at the funeral of his father, who died during her visit. The senior Rev. Buti had been a pioneer in the Black Dutch Reformed Church and a much-revered father of the church.

The significance of the visit by these RCA representatives had also been voiced the previous year by Rev. Allan Boesak when he addressed the Black Caucus as its keynote speaker.

The 1979 visit to South Africa by Smith and Hall, and the follow-up visit in 1980 by the President of the General Synod and the RCA Secretary for Africa, led to substantive actions by the Reformed Church in America to oppose the apartheid system. However, some in the denomination still applied their own criteria for how the struggle for justice and human dignity would be won in South Africa. They indicated that they would support only non-violent efforts for change. To put this view of things in proper perspective, one must ask whether those in the church who insisted—or still insist—on non-violent solutions to these intractable problems would apply the same standard to themselves if they were living under such inhumane conditions. Would they apply them even to their own government's military adventures in other parts of the world?

In 1986, the executive director of the RCA's Black Council was among a very few persons denied visas by the South African government to attend Bishop Desmond Tutu's enthronement as Archbishop of Cape Town.

The ongoing repression of moderate voices in South Africa would increasingly put the RCA in a position of either standing with more radical groups or remaining silent. After all that had happened after 1979, it was unlikely that the RCA could be silent in any case.

The denomination had gone on record in favor of the application of certain economic pressures against South Africa by the United Nations and the United States. If these pressures would not work and US business interests remained in apartheid South Africa, in a few years the RCA might have been faced with the challenge of opposing US military intervention on the side of the white minority government. Meanwhile, the church would do well to go on supporting the practice of Black South African students studying in the USA, especially those students who were recommended by anti-apartheid leaders, as well as the Belydende Kring, a courageous group of Black-led, Dutch Reformed anti-apartheid activists that took their stand at great risk.

The situation in South Africa changes daily. No doubt much

more will happen before these words are published and distributed.

The Southern Normal School

Some introductory facts about the Southern Normal School (SNS) appear in the (aforementioned) earlier book on the Black RCA experience by Noel Erskine. Erskine covered some of the school's positive history under the leadership of its founder, Mr. James Dooley. This institution has a glorious past and many of its alumni have done well in their chosen fields. Among their graduates is the president of a prestigious private college and the dean of one the country's major schools of law.

SNS's place in the history of Brewton, Alabama, is of particular importance for the town's Black population. The economy and the politics of Brewton, as in so many small towns in the South and elsewhere, are controlled by the town's wealthy white population. However, SNS is an institution which, in addition to the local Black churches, Black people founded. One can understand the school's importance to Blacks in the town only if this fact is fully comprehended. Most of the school's support came from the RCA, so SNS's pride as a school founded by Blacks has not been diminished by the fact that the RCA represents a group of "friendly white northerners." They are not of the same ilk, in the minds of Black Brewton residents, as local whites who have been guilty of or complicit in perpetrating segregation and overt racial discrimination.

Southern Normal was the primary source of Black pride and fond memories of the past for Brewton's Black community. And while, in its latter days, the school was not up to its old standards, it was nonetheless held in high esteem by the local Black population. To admit that SNS is not her old self would be to put in jeopardy the one independent symbol of Black achievement that Black people had in Brewton.

The truth of the matter is, though, that SNS was in a state of decline for several years. It was in search of its mission in a social context that was different from the one in which the school had been founded in the early years of the twentieth century.

Dooley and company started this school to meet the educational needs of Black children in the absence of a public-school option to meet the same needs. The school's traditional mission was challenged in earnest when desegregation came in the late sixties and early seventies. This development was the most serious of all challenges for SNS, because Black children could now attend schools with physical facilities that were superior to the best that SNS could offer. SNS understood itself as a Christian school and considered that, as such, it had something unique to offer its students. But the strength of this claim was tested time and time again when students, locally and elsewhere in Alabama, chose to attend public schools and when the cost of a SNS education continued to escalate.

The attraction of the public schools, because they were free, desegregated, and usually better equipped, forced SNS to rethink its role in order to continue attracting students. Would it become a school to provide terminal skills for students seeking employment immediately after graduating, thus abandoning the SNS tradition of preparing a sizable percentage of its students for liberal arts colleges? Would it become a school for troubled students from the big cities in the north? Or would it specialize in training the child who had difficulty adapting to the newly desegregated public-school system and who may have been "pushed out" by white teachers not willing to take the time to help the child overcome behavioral problems? These and other special functions for SNS have been contemplated — all in an effort to help it find a mission that would spark renewed purpose, enthusiasm, and support.

Although some changes have been made, the school still seems not to have settled entirely on what role it can and will play. This has resulted in some confusion and debate about how well it is doing its job. This debate emerged in 1969, the same year the Black Council was founded. That year, the Southern Normal School was being evaluated by the General Program Council, according to the normal procedure, to determine whether funding for the school's program should be continued. However, because there had been open questioning about the school's current mission, some wondered whether its evaluation might not lead to the school's closing.

The Black Council, as a whole, did not have much in-depth knowledge of SNS, but the Council became involved in advocating for the school shortly after the organization was launched.

SNS was a school for Black students and the Black Council was organized to address issues affecting the Black community, so it was natural for the Council to get involved. In its report to the General Synod in 1971, the Council said: "Additionally, the Black Council has significantly undergirded the life and program of Southern Normal School in Brewton, Alabama."

What this probably meant, since the Black Council had little or no access to much-needed financial assistance for the school, was that the Council had met with the school's administration and assured it that the Council intended to lend its moral support in the current period of evaluation. The RCA did not withdraw its support from the school after that evaluation, but it did decide that the school should come under the direction of an autonomous Board of Trustees.

Soon thereafter, a Board was organized and it included the first chairperson of the Black Council, B. Moses James. This Board functioned as a policy-making body of the institution, although the RCA was by far the largest single source of financial support. The new Board's first, most pressing responsibility was to determine what SNS's identity would be in light of its new circumstances. The school faced a critical point in its history, and there was no debating that it needed all the resources it could get its hands on to make the transition.

Things were not going well in 1973 when the Council held a full meeting in Brewton. The needs were tremendous, even with the substantial support that came from the RCA. It was surviving in large part because of its reputation and the sheer dedication of its faculty, some of whom had been at the school during its brighter days. The likelihood that additional support from the RCA would be forthcoming seemed slim and not much progress was being made to raise money from other sources. Just about every conceivable material need one might have in order to run a school effectively was in short supply. The one thing that people there seemed to have plenty of was dedication and determination. But even they had to admit this was not always enough.

Southern Normal School had a multi-dimensional profile. It has been indispensable to the identity of the Black community of Brewton. Another dimension that deserves attention is how its relationship to the RCA, a denomination unfamiliar to most southern Blacks, affected its development as a school for Black people in Alabama. The school attracted Black students from throughout the state. Yet, while it regarded itself as a Christian school, very few of its graduates have pursued Christian ministry as a vocation. The Reverend Samuel Williams was the only graduate who became a minister in the RCA. Black people took advantage of its program, but Alabama's considerable Black leadership seemed to have little sense of responsibility for the school's survival or well-being. It may well be that Black people's lack of familiarity with the RCA has allowed a certain distance and lack of relatedness that is not good for the school's long-term future. Cultivating this sense of responsibility for the school, which has played no small part in the development of Black leadership in the State of Alabama, is still a challenge to be met.

The fact that SNS remained a "special project" of the RCA, and thus isolated from the mainstream Black population of the State, made a critical difference in the school's apparent unreadiness for the demanding future it faced.

The decision of the RCA to come to the aid of Mr. Dooley when the SNS had fallen on hard times was presumably motivated by good intentions. The very survival of the school and its subsequent physical expansion is due to the RCA's commitment. Why did the students at this school remain so apparently untouched by the church that supported it? Was the RCA seen in such foreign terms that Black people thought little of becoming a part of it? These questions, although not easily answered, are important to those who would try to comprehend the school's lingering troubles.

Is this a case where the denomination wanted to have a positive relationship with the Black community, but was hampered by its own members' lack of familiarity with or contact with Black people? Perhaps the whites in the RCA were doing things the best they could. And the way their benevolence was sometimes received did not help them get beyond their generous paternalistic disposition.

Black folk have been guilty from time to time of being "overly appreciative." They have genuflected and "tommed" more than once in the face of their white donors and benefactors. How were the whites to know that this was customary deception among Black folk who felt they had to engage in such behavior in order to survive? This manner of behaving—with the white person being the earnest, goodhearted giver and the Black person the servile, deferential recipient—has hurt the prospects of racial reconciliation because it does not allow people to see one another as they really are. The whites go away thinking themselves superior, while the Blacks, having acted inferior for so long, find it hard to distinguish between genuine good will and its artificial, superficial facsimilie. For as long as it lasts, people who treat each other this way can appear to have a "good thing going," but, one day, the failure to be honest with one another will likely come back to haunt them.

This is part of what has happened with the Southern Normal School. The situation has elements of the classic "ham and egg" story.[21] For the RCA, SNS was making a contribution to the Black community, but it was not clear whether the school's survival was a matter that would inspire the Black Alabamian's total commitment. A new sense of ownership and access to the RCA, and to the Board of Trustees, on the part of these citizens had to develop, and vice-versa.

In 1974, a group of persons meeting informally, during the recess of a Black Caucus session, discussed complaints that were brought before it by persons with direct experience of the school and its administration. They concluded, after a long discussion, that the school's leader should resign. The discussion was precipitated by two events. The first was the conclusion of a review of the school by the RCA's General Program Council, which found the school in relatively good health save for a few needed minor adjustments. This was a conclusion with which several persons present at the Caucus

---

21   One morning a chicken and a pig were out for a walk. The chicken suggested they have breakfast and proposed a menu of ham and eggs. The pig thought it easy enough for the chicken to suggest ham and eggs because for the chicken such a breakfast only required a contribution, but for the pig it required a total commitment.

disagreed. Secondly, at the meeting of the Caucus, a mother whose child had been dismissed from the school for alleged misconduct reported that her son had been sent home to New Jersey by bus without her having been notified. This mother's statement to the Caucus opened a floodgate of discontent expressed by people who had not been outspoken about the school prior to that time.

Because the Black Council was presumed to be in agreement with this action, from that point on, the Council was thought to be opposed to the school leader and his administration. All subsequent efforts made by the Council to encourage improvement at the school, especially in the face of the many concerns that were directed to the Council by a number of people, were met with the suspicion that the Council's real aim was the school leader's ouster.

The Council's formal view was that charges against SNS's leader could be damaging to the school and that, if such accusations were without foundation, they should be summarily refuted. That is why the Council advocated open and fair means of resolving the school's internal problems.

During the period of controversy that began in the early 1970s, the Black Council felt it had a responsibility to help seek some resolution of the apparent problems at SNS. In 1981, the Black Caucus invited the chairperson of the SNS Board to share her views on how the Board was dealing with the school's problems. Her presentation did not allay the growing criticism. Instead, criticism grew to the point that, in the spring of 1983, the Board of Trustees felt it necessary to give the school's director a vote of confidence. By this time, however, the Classis of Florida, to which the now defunct Bergen Memorial Church in Brewton was related, had independently determined reasons for questioning the Board's action. Therefore, the Classis called upon the General Program Council to undertake a hearing on the issues that were being raised. The Black Council supported this action by the GPC because it saw this as an excellent chance for SNS to clear the air and get a fresh start in the best interests of the children. The school simply could not continue under a growing cloud of doubt about its integrity.

There is a definite need for the type of school SNS aspires to be, operating according to the tenets of the Christian faith. But a serious effort must be made to determine what needs this school can best meet currently, given the changing educational options for Black people in the Brewton area and beyond. In order to do this with maximum effectiveness, the RCA must send signals to the area's Black citizens that it is eager to have their input in helping to determine this role. Here is where the Black Council can play a constructive role.

Meanwhile, the challenge to RCA members who supported the school in the past and who might be willing to support it in the days to come was to accept the changing role that SNS must adopt. The Black Council believed the school's future role deserved the full support of the church. For those who have not come to grips with the imperative for broader involvement by Black Alabamians in particular, the emerging SNS may be hard to accept. Yet, unless steps along these lines are taken, SNS will have less and less appeal. A hopeful sign that the future will be faced with diligence, integrity, and creativity lies in the school's new executive leadership. Mrs. Mary Humphrey, the school's acting director, and Mrs. Pauline Williams, its Board chairperson, have outlined plans to restore the school to a semblance of its past preeminence.

The Urban Ministry Policy Statement

In 1977, Isaac Rottenberg prepared the first draft of a proposed policy statement on Urban Ministry for consideration by the RCA's General Program Council. This draft was criticized by the Black Council, the Hispanic Council, and the Council on Pacific and Asian Ministries because its basic effect would be the continuation of the cycle of dependence by churches attended by people of color. The statement sought to reclaim for "Urban Ministry" a place of visibility in the denomination, which would encourage potential contributors to give money to projects that white pastors saw fit to introduce and support in communities where racial minorities lived. The Black Council believed developing a new policy gave the RCA an opportunity to distance itself from the practice of providing endless financial support to dependent congregations and to support ministries not linked directly to congregations. It also presented the church with an opportunity to affirm the development of self-reliant, local congregations as the centerpiece of the RCA's witness in Black communities.

The disagreements over the direction the new policy statement would take resulted in its delay for several months. The GPC devoted a full meeting to the subject. Those who supported the initial direction of the proposed policy insisted that the term "urban" went far beyond churches located in Black and Hispanic neighborhoods. Yet, virtually every slide presentation and every speech given at the GPC meeting in relation to the policy made reference to Black and Hispanic peoples. Urban Ministry, then, was just a code word. A group of white pastors in the New York area were the most aggressive leaders of the effort to have the GPC raise money for the "inner city." Black pastors who had been associated with them in the beginning soon drifted away when they saw the implications of their advocacy

There was nothing sinister about the position of these white ministers; their thinking was simply a holdover from the days when it was presumed that Black folk could not carry the weight of maintaining their own churches. Aid was sought from elsewhere by these pastors because, ·otherwise, they feared, the doors of the churches would be closed. This view was touched upon earlier, during our discussion of how the cycle of dependence got its start, with leading Black lay people encouraging dependence by their own lack of vision and by their lack of faith in themselves to manage with what they had.

In addition to the special session of the GPC, a conference involving urban ministry stakeholders was held, to explore issues in depth. This conference met in Richfield, Ohio, and it gave participants an opportunity to put all the tough perspectives on the table. The stakeholders consisted largely of whites who had pioneered the RCA's racial transition from white to Black congregations in neighborhoods that were largely Black, as well as the emerging non-white leadership in the denomination.

It was inevitable that some serious disagreements would arise in this meeting, the most insulting of which was the theological reflection that was given by Rev. Jim Van Hoven, who accused the racial minority councils of not being progressive *enough*. He claimed they focused their attention not upon issues of suffering in the world, but rather upon issues like representation in the RCA.

This was a grossly inaccurate reading of the issues that the councils had been addressing in their work, but the implication that it was not important for racial minority groups to confront the RCA with its own institutional racism rendered the presenter uncredible. Rev. Van Hoven's remarks represented the thinking of white liberal advocates for the Black cause and illustrated the chasm that separated the two groups. It was in this kind of situation that one could see the sharp distinction between sympathetic support and a commitment to self-determination. It is a harsh distinction which, once made, can often cause lots of pain, because the truth will be exposed about those who have considered themselves natural friends.

After Richfield, the controversy continued. A drafting committee was set up to develop a new policy statement for GPC to consider. This time, it was a group effort and the chairperson of the drafting committee was one the leaders of the Black Council, the Rev. Earle N.S. Hall. The draft policy statement that was produced by this committee, after some tough dialogue and negotiation, won the approval of the GPC, the Black Council, and, ultimately, the General Synod.

At the heart of the policy statement development process was the issue of dependence versus self-reliance. Could congregations of Black and Hispanic people really be self-determining in the RCA, or would they always be in the position of relying on their white friends to pay their way? While the policy statement supports self-reliance and discourages efforts to perpetuate dependence, this debate is far from over. Putting the debate to rest will depend upon whether Black people themselves regard the challenge of self-reliance seriously enough to achieve it. To reach this goal, in some instances, will require numerical growth. The kind of leadership that a church will need in order to build a numerically larger congregation will be increasingly important where active membership is declining.

Report to the General Synod

As it is the responsibility of the Black Council to report to the General Synod each year on matters of particular concern to the church's Black members, several important matters of a Social Justice nature were brought to the Synod's attention. During the 1970s–1980s, the list of such concerns has grown. Among them are: (1) support for a national holiday honoring Martin Luther King, Jr.; (2) the need for a government policy that guarantees a job to every person who wants to work; (3) the extent of racism's pervasiveness in the media; and (4) the impact of budget cuts and other policies of the Reagan Administration on the gains made by Black people over the past two decades. In addition to these and other societal concerns, or course, the matter of participation of racial minority peoples in the affairs of the church and the issue of South Africa have been constant themes of the Black Council's reports to the General Synod.

The Black Council Is Committed to Unity

A statement that the Black Council is committed to unity will raise eyebrows in disbelief among some in the denomination, because they see the Council as a source of constant controversy and disunity. For such persons, the essence of unity is the absence of conflict, a façade of good relations without regard for the chasm of ignorance and alienation that actually separates people in their daily lives, whether by race, economic status, gender, or national tradition. From its beginning, the Council has tried to create a greater appreciation of the basis for community. It has sought the kind of community that grows out of the common life that all people share. If the common life is experienced so unequally by different people, the possibility of their experiencing true unity is nil. In order to find genuine community, this inequality must be candidly confronted and overcome, not ignored or denied.

That is why the Council applauds the RCA's membership in the National and World Councils of Churches. These organizations, whatever their imperfections, see the struggle for Christian unity as inseparable from the struggle to overcome the disparities that divide people in the economic, political, social, and cultural spheres. In the National Council of Churches (NCC), it has been thus far the privilege of three members of the Black Council to serve on the RCA delegation to the NCC's Governing Board. These are the late B. Moses

James, Anna Gonzales, and Sara Smith. Nida Thomas, one of the founding members of the Black Council, has served on the NCC's Personnel Committee. The Black Council's Executive Director (this writer) served as an NCC officer for seven years, first as a program vice-president, then as president.

The World Council of Churches, and especially its Programme to Combat Racism, has been affirmed publicly by the Black Council on a number of occasions. In addition to giving support to its executive director while he served as Moderator for the WCC's PCR Commission, the Black Council made financial contributions to the PCR's Special Fund. This support continued after the RCA was forbidden by act of the General Synod from making such contributions. The Council also hosted the PCR's staff director in one of its official sessions.

In each instance when the RCA was asked to consider an overture to withdraw as a member of either the NCC or the WCC, the Black Council has associated the opposition to these ecumenical organizations with the same mindset that has opposed the Council itself. Both Councils of Churches—the NCC and the WCC—are criticized by conservative churches and individuals largely because of their modest efforts in aiding oppressed peoples to achieve their dignity and human rights. Such work by ecumenical organizations has been labelled too political, but to the Black Council these actions are considered faithful to the gospel of Christ. The church has long expressed with words its concern for the poor, so when a church or a group of churches actually *does* something to demonstrate their commitment to the poor, is it not a cause for rejoicing? The perspective that makes persons intolerant of other Christian traditions and people of other faiths resembles in kind the intolerance that manifests itself as bigotry toward persons of color.

The Black Council considers itself an integral part of the

ecumenical movement. From its early days, it has supported organizations that encourage inter-denominational cooperation among Black people. Most notable among these is the National Conference of Black Churchmen, on whose Board the Council's first chairperson and its executive director served. The Black Council was also involved in the creation of an organization of Black church executives who worked in predominantly white denominations, called Black Executives in Denominations, Related Organizations and Communions (BEDROC). In all these groups, the operating assumption was the same: Reconciliation can take place only among those who understand deeply that the destiny of the earth and its inhabitants is intertwined and interdependent.

Envisioning the Future

In all that the Black Council has done in well over of decade of work, it has been guided by the aforementioned principle of reconciliation—that a peer relationship among all church members is essential for the integrity of the church. This understanding is biblically rooted and seen as an indispensable aspect of the faith of those who claim Christ as Lord and Savior.

For the first five years of the organization's existence, much of its time was spent organizing the Caucus and determining its priorities. This led the Council to the conclusion that *self-reliance* of congregations in predominantly Black communities; that *leadership development opportunities* for the laity and the clergy; and that *open, frank dialogue* between Blacks and whites are *essential ingredients* of the reconciling process that the Council envisions for the RCA and for society at-large.

This process is not one in which disagreement never happens. It is not one that avoids making participants ill at ease. Nor is it a process that is so innocuous that it has no implications for the sharing of power and for changing institutional structures. It is, however, a process that is based upon love, a love that has lasting and sometimes costly human consequences.

Many white members of the RCA who want to do their fair share to create a conducive environment for this brand of reconciliation should affirm the importance of the Black religious experience for the whole church and resist a highly individualistic understanding of Christian life. The latter has inadequate regard for the systemic barriers that go beyond the personal realm to keep people divided. It must be kept in mind that one's socio-economic circumstances largely determines one's view of how the gospel should be applied.

Enticing Black people to accept aid or refusing to assist them in their efforts to become self-reliant is contrary to the long-term interests of these churches and of the RCA.

It is not a threat to the Reformed tradition that "new" peoples are joining the RCA. It is rather an opportunity to bear witness to the stated will of God that we shall all be one (John 17:21), without regard to culture, creed, race, or tongue (Galatians 3:28). Believing in this without feeling the need to mold the "weaker parts" (1 Cor 12:20-27) into one's own image is the challenge of the cross. Black people must alter their behavior and thinking too. They must stop pretending that their prior religious heritage does not matter. They must resolve to develop a realistic plan for becoming self-reliant and must be determined to take full part in the life of the church beyond the congregational level. Neither Blacks or whites can forego understanding the struggle for reconciliation and unity in biblical terms. The work of the Black Council is an integral part of the mission of the church, not an isolated part of it. Council members must be empowered by this understanding of the gospel to confront and surmount the walls that divide sisters and brothers in the faith, one from another.

Making these commitments and being careful to adhere to them will yield a harvest of Black congregations in the future that can give leadership to the denomination in ministry with people in local situations. Congregations in situations of economic poverty and racism will become more effective in their witness and they will be better able to offer insights into how the whole church, acting together, can "wrestle with principalities and powers" (Ephesians 6:12).

Perhaps the RCA was late in coming into a relationship with the Black community, compared to several other historic American denominations; but, quite apart from the drifting that characterized this relationship in earlier decades, today, all of its component parts—"red and yellow, black and white"—are present, and are determined to be *bona fide* RCA members.

This has been seen by some as a disruption, an inconvenience to the smooth functioning of the business of the church. It has been regarded as an unhelpful addition to the ongoing and emerging internal problems of the denomination, thus recalling the earlier frame of mind in the 18th and 19th centuries. But to others, it has been embraced as the gift from God that it is—a new and exciting opportunity for the RCA to renew itself by reflecting the diversity of God's rainbow of humanity and to be an example of how the walls that might normally divide us can, through Christ, be broken down.

APPENDIX

Appendix I. Credo on Race Relations

CREDO ON RACE RELATIONS

As prepared and recommended by Christian Action Commission of General Synod of the Reformed Church in America.

Adopted at the General Synod held at Buck Hill Falls, Pa., June 7, 1957.

    I. **We believe** that the problem of race is a problem of human relations. We believe that the Scriptures of the Old and New Testaments provide the final authority for all matters of human relations. We believe that all problems of human existence are resolved in the love for God above all, and for our neighbor as ourselves. We further believe that such love has been fully revealed to us in the life and work of Jesus Christ, our Lord and Saviour; and that the grace to participate in that love is readily available through the Holy Spirit by faith. We believe that the primary function of the Church of Jesus Christ is to witness to that love to all people in every walk of life.

    II. **We believe** that in the light of the Biblical revelation, we have fallen short in the demonstration of that love. We hereby make an act of confession and repentance for:

    1—our insensitivity to the needs of others.

    2—our acquiescence through silence in a sub-christian social pattern which denies the full rights of human dignity to some minority groups within our national borders.

    3—our failure to realize the mission of the Church in our own communities, while advancing the Church's mission at a distance.

    4—our persistence in pursuing the historical pattern of ethnic exclusivism in the face of the mounting pressures of social heterogeneity.

    5—our emotional prejudices which often sap our spiritual vitality and snap our moral nerve.

For these and other acts and attitudes, Gracious Lord, forgive us.

    III. **We believe** that sincere repentance manifests itself in acts of obedient love. We, therefore, believe that our sincerity will be demonstrated through concrete local acts, such as:

    1—identification with minority groups victimized through unjust discrimination.

    2—conscientious efforts to open the doors of all churches to all people.

3—the support of those laws and agencies designed to uphold and guarantee the rights and
health of all.
4—the promotion of inter-group discussions, where
in atmospheres of understanding and good-will,
the forces for reconciliation may operate
creatively.
5—the education of our youth in the privileges and
responsibilities of life in a free, mixed society.

IV. **We believe** that Christian love represents the highest criterion
for all human relations. In its light, all personal
relations are judged; through its power, all ten-
sions in race relations can be resolved. We believe also, that in a responsible society, the immediate goals of such love will be structured into
laws. We believe that the Church exercises its
prophetic role when it inspires its constituent
society to construct such laws, and when it subjects such laws to the scrutiny of Divine revelation. In that spirit, we believe that the recent
Supreme Court decision on the ordered, gradual
desegregation of the public schools of our land,
represents an effective legal expression of Christian attitudes and convictions at the present time.
We believe that we should support and implement
the intent and content of that decision.

V. **We believe** that many difficulties dog the steps of the effective reconciliation of the races in our day, not
least of which is the problem of inter-marriage.
We believe that this emotionally charged issue is
often used by Christian people to becloud clearly
perceived Christian responsibilities. We believe,
also, that disproportionate emphasis has been
placed on this aspect of the problem of race relations. We further believe that when the problem
is sincerely presented, sober reflection is in order.
We believe that the origin of the races is obscured
in antiquity; that neither Scriptural revelation
nor scientific investigation has been able to pene-
trate that obscurity. We, therefore, believe that
the will of God cannot be identified dogmatically
or exclusively either with the maintenance of the
separation of the races or with the amalgamation
of the races.

We believe that marriage is a Divinely appointed
institution to perpetuate the human race, to pre-

of property are subservient to the needs of people.
We believe that there is nothing inherent in race
differences to necessitate the decline in property
values. We believe that restrictive pressures and
flight-in-panic on the part of dominant groups often
lead to unnecessary real estate declines and contribute to the establishment and perpetuation of
ghetto-existence.

VIII. **We believe** that Christians should actively support those
groups or agencies which are striving to achieve
social justice; especially those which do so from
Christian motives. We commend the method of
non-violent resistance as an effective immediate
demonstration of the power of Christian suffering
love. We believe that the church acts in the Spirit
when, through continuous intercessory prayer, it
strengthens the power of this expression of Christian righteousness.

IX. **We believe** that the problem of race relations in our day presents to the Church splendid opportunities to make
effective witness to the energizing power of Christian grace which we have found in Jesus Christ.
We believe that the basic problem resides not in
society, but in the individual soul. If a house divided against itself cannot stand, how much less
can a soul divided against itself? We believe that
through the Gospel of Reconciliation, Christ unites
divided souls. We further believe that in His
grace are resources sufficient to conquer deeply-
rooted emotional prejudices, and to transform di-
visive customs into patterns of social cohesion.

X. **We believe** that each generation inherits from the past problems for which it cannot be held directly account-
able, but for whose solutions it is held responsible.
We believe that race relations is such a problem.
We believe that the Cross of Christ, seen as vicarious atonement, points the way to the Christian
resolution of this dilemma. We believe that we
are called to bear the wounds (or crosses) of
vicarious suffering, so that the least of Christ's
brethren may find their rightful places in the
society of men and the Kingdom of God.

Appendix II. The Black Manifesto
The Black Economic Development Conference

We the black people assembled in Detroit, Michigan for the National Black Economic Development Conference are fully aware that we have been forced to come together because racist white America has exploited our resources, our minds, our bodies, our labor. For centuries we have been forced to live as colonized people inside the United States, victimized by the most vicious, racist system in the world. We have helped to build the most industrial country in the world.

We are therefore demanding of the white Christian churches and Jewish synagogues which are part and parcel of the system of capitalism, that they begin to pay reparations to black people in this country. We are demanding $500,000,000 from the Christian white churches and the Jewish synagogues. This total comes to 15 dollars per nigger. This is a low estimate for we maintain there are probably more than 30,000,000 black people in this country. $15 a nigger is not a large sum of money and we know that the churches and synagogues have a tremendous wealth and its membership, white America, has profited and still exploits black people. We are also not unaware that the exploitation of colored peoples around the world is aided and abetted by the white Christian churches and synagogues. This demand for $500,000,000 is not an idle resolution or empty words. Fifteen dollars for every black brother and sister in the United States is only a beginning of the reparations due us as people who have been exploited and degraded, brutalized, killed and persecuted. Underneath all of this exploitation, the racism of this country has produced a psychological effect upon us that we are beginning to shake off. We are no longer afraid to demand our full rights as a people in this decadent society.

106

We are demanding $500,000,000 to be spent in the following way:

1. We call for the establishment of a Southern land bank to help our brothers and sisters who have to leave their land because of racist pressure for people who want to establish cooperative farms, but who have no funds. We have seen too many farmers evicted from their homes because they have dared to defy the white racism of this country. We need money for land. We must fight for massive sums of money for this Southern Land Bank. We call for $200,000,000 to implement this program.

2. We call for the establishment of four major publishing and printing industries in the United States to be funded with ten million dollars each. These publishing houses are to be located in Detroit, Atlanta, Los Angeles, and New York. They will help to generate capital for further cooperative investments in the black community, provide jobs and an alternative to the white-dominated and controlled printing field.

3. We call for the establishment of four of the most advanced scientific and futuristic audio-visual networks to be located in Detroit, Chicago, Cleveland and Washington, D.C. These TV networks will provide an alternative to the racist propaganda that fills the current television networks. Each of these TV networks will be funded by ten million dollars each.

4. We call for a research skills center which will provide research on the problems of black people. This center must be funded with no less than 30 million dollars.

5. We call for the establishment of a training center for the teaching of skills in community organization, photography, movie making, television making and repair, radio building and repair and all other skills

needed in communication. This training center shall be funded with no less than ten million dollars.

6. We recognize the role of the National Welfare Rights Organization and we intend to work with them. We call for ten million dollars to assist in the organization of welfare recipients. We want to organize the welfare workers in this country so that they may demand more money from the government and better administration of the welfare system of this country.

7. We call for $20,000,000 to establish a National Black Labor Strike and Defense Fund. This is necessary for the protection of black workers and their families who are fighting racist working conditions in this country.

We call for the establishment of the International Black Appeal (IBA). This International Black Appeal will be funded with no less than $20,000,000. The IBA is charged with producing more capital for the establishment of cooperative businesses in the United States and in Africa, our Motherland. The International Black Appeal is one of the most important demands that we are making for we know that it can generate and raise funds throughout the United States and help our African brothers. The IBA is charged with three functions and shall be headed by James Forman:

(a) Raising money for the program of the National Black Economic Development Conference.
(b) The development of cooperatives in African countries and support of African Liberation movements
(c) Establishment of a Black Anti-Defamation League which will protect our African image.
   1. We call for the establishment of a Black University to be funded with $130,000,000 to be located in the South. Negotiations are presently under way with a Southern University.

2.   We demand that IFCO allocate all unused funds in the planning budget to implement the demands of this conference.

In order to win our demands we are aware that we will have to have massive support, therefore:

(1) We call upon all black people throughout the United States to consider themselves as members of the National Black Economic Development Conference and to act in unity to help force the racist white Christian churches and Jewish synagogues to implement these demands.

(2) We call upon all the concerned black people across the country to contact black workers, black women, black students and black unemployed, community groups, welfare organizations, teacher organizations, church leaders and organizations, explaining how these demands are vital to the black community of the U.S. Pressure by whatever means necessary should be applied to the white power structure of the racist white Christian churches and Jewish synagogues. All black people should act boldly in confronting our white oppressors and demanding this modest reparation of 15 dollars per black man.

(3) Delegates and members of the National Black Economic Development Conference are urged to call press conferences in the cities and to attempt to get as many black organizations as possible to support the demands of the conference. The quick use of the press in the local areas will heighten the tension and these demands must be attempted to be won in a short period of time, although we are prepared for protracted and long range struggle.

(4) We call for the total disruption of selected church sponsored agencies operating anywhere in the U.S. and

109

the world. Black workers, black women, black students and the black unemployed are encouraged to seize the offices, telephones, and printing apparatus of all church sponsored agencies and to hold these in trusteeship until our demands are met.

(5) We call upon all delegates and members of the National Black Economic Development Conference to stage sit-in demonstrations at selected black and white churches. This is not to be interpreted as a continuation of the sit-in movement of the early sixties but we know that active confrontation inside white churches is possible and will strengthen the possibility of meeting our demands. Such confrontation can take the form of reading the Black Manifesto instead of a sermon or passing it out to church members. The principle of self-defense should be applied if attacked.

(6) On May 4, 1969 or a date thereafter, depending upon local conditions, we call upon black people to commence the disruption of the racist churches and synagogues throughout the United States.

(7) We call upon IFCO to serve as a central staff to coordinate the mandate of the conference and to reproduce and distribute en mass literature, leaflets, news items, press releases and other material.

(8) We call upon all delegates to find within the white community those forces which will work under the leadership of blacks to implement these demands by whatever means necessary. By taking such actions, white Americans will demonstrate concretely that they are willing to fight the white skin privilege and the white supremacy and racism which has forced us as black people to make these demands.

(9) We call upon all white Christians and Jews to practice patience, tolerance, understanding, and nonviolence as they have encouraged, advised and demanded that we as black people should do throughout our entire

110

enforced slavery in the United States. The true test of their faith and belief in the Cross and the words of the prophets will certainly be put to a test as we seek legitimate and extremely modest reparations for our role in developing the industrial base of the Western world through our slave labor. But we are no longer slaves, we are men and women, proud of our African heritage, determined to have our dignity.

(10) We are so proud of our African heritage and realize concretely that our struggle is not only to make revolution in the United States, but to protect our brothers and sisters in Africa and to help them rid themselves of racism, capitalism, and imperialism by whatever means necessary, including armed struggle. We are and must be willing to fight the defamation of our African image wherever it rears its ugly head. We are therefore charging the Steering Committee to create a Black Anti-Defamation League to be funded by money raised from the International Black Appeal.

(11) We fully recognize that revolution in the United States and Africa, our Motherland, is more than a one dimensional operation. It will require the total integration of the political, economic, and military components and therefore, we call upon all our brothers and sisters who have acquired training and expertise in the fields of engineering, electronics, research, community organization, physics, biology, chemistry, mathematics, medicine, military science and warfare to assist the National Black Economic Development Conference in the implementation of its program.

(12) To implement these demands we must have a fearless leadership. We must have a leadership which is willing to battle the church establishment to implement these demands. To win our demands we will have to declare war on the white Christian churches and synagogues

and this means we may have to fight the government structure of this country. Let no one her think that these demands will be met by our mere stating them. For the sake of the churches and synagogues, we hope that they have the wisdom to understand that these demands are modest and reasonable. But if the white Christians and Jews are not willing to meet our demands through peace and good will, then we declare war and we are prepared to fight by whatever means necessary....

Brothers and sisters, we no longer are shuffling our feet and scratching our heads. We are tall, black and proud.

And we say to the white Christian churches and Jewish synagogues, to the government of this country and to all the white racist imperialists who compose it, there is only one thing left that you can do to further degrade black people and that is to kill us. But we have been dying too long for this country. We have died in every war. We are dying in Vietnam today fighting the wrong enemy.

The new black man wants to live and to live means that we must not become static or merely believe in self-defense. We must boldly go out and attack the white Western world at its power centers. The white Christian churches are another form of government in this country and they are used by the government of this country to exploit the people of Latin America, Asia and Africa, but the day is soon coming to an end. Therefore, brothers and sisters, the demands we make upon the white Christian churches and the Jewish synagogues are small demands. They represent 15 dollars per black person in these United States. We can legitimately demand this from the church power structure. We must demand more from the United States Government.

But to win our demands from the church which is linked up with the United States Government, we must not forget that it will ultimately be by force and power that we will win.

We are not threatening the churches. We are saying that we know the churches came with the military might of the colonizers and have been sustained by the military might of the colonizers. Hence, if the churches in colonial territories were established by military might, we know deep within our hearts that we must be prepared to use force to get our demands. We are not saying that this is the road we want to take. It is not, but let us be very clear that we are not opposed to force and we are not opposed to violence. We were captured in Africa by violence. We were kept in bondage and political servitude and forced to work as slaves by the military machinery and the Christian church working hand in hand.

We recognize that in issuing this manifesto we must prepare for a long range educational campaign in all communities of this country, but we know that the Christian churches have contributed to our oppression in white America. We do not intend to abuse our black brothers and sisters in black churches who have uncritically accepted Christianity. We want them to understand how the racist white christian church with its hypocritical declarations and doctrines of brotherhood has abused our trust and faith. An attack on the religious beliefs of black people is not our major objective, even though we know that we were not Christians, when we were brought to this country, but that Christianity was used to help enslave us. Our objective in issuing this Manifesto is to force the racist white Christian Church to begin the payment of reparations which are due to all black people, not only by the Church but also by private business and the U.S. government. We see this focus on the Christian Church as an effort around which all black people can unite.

Our demands are negotiable, but they cannot be

minimized, they can only be increased and the Church is asked to come up with larger sums of money than we are asking. Our slogans are:

ALL ROADS MUST LEAD TO REVOLUTION
UNITE WITH WHOMEVER YOU CAN UNITE
NEUTRALIZE WHEREVER POSSIBLE
FIGHT OUR ENEMIES RELENTLESSLY
VICTORY TO THE PEOPLE
LIFE AND GOOD HEALTH TO MANKIND
RESISTANCE TO DOMINATION BY THE WHITE CHRISTIAN CHURCHES AND THE JEWISH SYNAGOGUES
REVOLUTIONARY BLACK POWER
WE SHALL WIN WITHOUT A DOUBT

April, 1969

BIBLIOGRAPHY

Erskine, Noel Leo. *Black People and the Reformed Church in America.* New York: Reformed Church in America, 1978.

Lecky, Robert S. and Wright, H. Elliott. *Black Manifesto: Religion, Racism and Reparations.* New York: Sheed & Ward, 1969.

Reformed Church in America. *Minutes of the General Synod.* New York: The Reformed Church in America, 1956, 1959, 1960, 1963, 1964, 1965, 1967, 1969, 1978.

Wilmore, Gayraud S. *The Church's Response to the Black Manifesto.* A paper written for the United Presbyterian Church, 1969.

INDEX

D

E

F

G

H

I